FREE BOOK BONUS

Because Medicare is so confusing and because everyone learns differently, we created a special BOOK BONUS to help you get your Medicare decisions right the first time.

The best news? Access to the site is complete free for everyone who purchases this book.

You can find details about how to access the book bonus in Chapter 12.

Here is what the book bonus includes:

- a Medicare toolkit complete with helpful checklists, flowcharts, PDF guides, and links to important Medicare forms that you may need.
- a custom Medicare calendar that calculates your Medicare IEP based on your birthday. It lists all the other enrollment periods you'll need to know as well.
- top-secret, never-before-seen videos that I filmed solely for readers of this book to increase your knowledge on a few key topics.

"Danielle is the pro that other pros reach out to when they have questions about Medicare (myself included!). Whenever a listener asks a question about a Medicare related topic, Danielle's resources are the first place I check. Avoiding costly Medicare mistakes is crucial to the financial security of retiring Americans, and Danielle's new book will teach you how to deftly maneuver this complicated topic."

—**Benjamin J. Brandt, CFP, RICP & host of**
the *Retirement Starts Today* Podcast

"Avoiding Medicare penalties and pitfalls is an important step in protecting your retirement nest egg. This book pulls out all the stops to help you do that and so much more. It's a must have for anyone who will eventually retire."

—**Ellie Kay, co-host of The Money Millhouse**
podcast and author of 15 books

"Danielle has written the perfect primer to help me make informed annual plan decisions for my mother. Soon I will be eligible for Medicare and this easy to understand book will be my go-to resource for preventing mistakes and making my own informed decision."

—**Debra Hallisey, *author of Your Caregiver Relationship Contract***

"Danielle Roberts has created the go-to resource for people who want to understand the ins and outs of Medicare and to avoid the mistakes made by so many over the years. I have been a financial advisor for over 25 years and am glad to finally have a resource on Medicare we can recommend to our clients. In '10 Costly Medicare Mistakes You Can't Afford to Make," Danielle lifts the veil of complexity and shines a light on best practices to help readers get the most out of Medicare from start to finish. I highly recommend this book!"

—**Eric D. Brotman, CFP, CEO of BFG Financial Advisors,**
podcast host, and author of *Don't Retire...Graduate!*

10 CO$TLY

MEDICARE
MISTAKES

You Can't Afford to Make

10 CO$TLY MEDICARE MISTAKES

You Can't Afford to Make

DANIELLE KUNKLE ROBERTS

R SELANE
PUBLISHING

ISBN 978-1-7353786-1-9

PUBLISHING

2601 Meacham Blvd #500
Fort Worth, TX 76137
https://tenmedicaremistakes.com

This book does not replace the advice of an insurance agent. Consult a Medicare broker before making your plan selections.

First Edition: September 2020

To my grandparents, Bernard and Ruth Roland

Contents

Introduction   *xix*

Part 1—The Basics

CHAPTER 1: Medicare Mistake #1: Assuming that   3
Medicare Is Free

Medicare Mistake #1: Assuming Medicare Is Free   3
Understanding Medicare Starts with the Parts   5
Medicare Is Far from Free   10
Medicare Costs AND Cost-Sharing Expenses   13
Your Premiums for Medicare Part A   15
Your Premiums for Medicare Part B   17
Your Premiums for Medicare Parts C and D   21
Key Takeaways   24

CHAPTER 2: Medicare Mistake #2: Expecting   27
Medicare to Cover 100% of Your Health-Care Costs

Medicare Mistake #2: Expecting that Medicare   28
Will Cover 100% of Your Health-Care Costs
in Retirement
Common Terms   28
Medicare Cost-Sharing Expenses: What Do You Pay   30
for as You Go?
Your Part A Cost-Sharing Expenses   31
Your Part B Cost-Sharing Expenses   36
Your Part D Cost-Sharing Expenses   39
What Expenses Does Medicare not Cover?   39

Medicare vs. Medicaid   43

Key Takeaways   45

Part II—Major Decision:
When Is Your Best Time to Enroll?

CHAPTER 3: Medicare Mistake #3: Missing Your   49
Initial Enrollment Period (IEP)

Medicare Mistake #3: Missing Your Initial   50
Enrollment Period (IEP)

Your Initial Enrollment Period for Medicare   50

Your Medicare Start Date   53

Medicare and Employer Coverage   57

Active Large-Employer Coverage: 20 or More   57
Employees

Small-Employer Coverage: Under 20 Employees   65

Recap: Medicare and Employer Coverage   68

Retiree Coverage   69

Individual Coverage through the Affordable Care   76
Act (ACA)

What if You Can't Afford Medicare?   78

Key Takeaways   79

Part III—Major Decision:
Will You Need Prescription Drug Coverage?

CHAPTER 4: Medicare Mistake #4: Skipping Part D   85
without Having other Coverage

Medicare Mistake #4: Skipping Part D without   86
Having other Coverage

Part D is Optional. Sort Of.   87

The Four Phases of Part D   94

What Is the "Tier Structure" for Part D Drug Plans?   95

How Do the Four Phases Work?   96

All Drug Plans Have Minimum Standards   101

What Drugs Fall outside of Part D?   101

Conditional Approval   102

How Do You Choose a Part D Drug Plan?   104

Managing Part D   106

Key Takeaways   107

CHAPTER 5: Medicare Mistake #5: Failing to Keep and Submit Proof of Your Creditable Coverage   109

The Certificate of Creditable Coverage   110

Medicare Mistake #5: Failing to Keep and Submit Proof of Your Creditable Coverage   110

Why Do People Miss the Notice of Late Penalty?   112

Key Takeaways   114

Exhibit 5-1. Sample Notice of Late-Enrollment Penalty for Part D   115

Exhibit 5-2. Declaration of Prior Prescription Drug Coverage   116

Exhibit 5-3. Sample Certificate of Creditable Coverage   117

Part IV—Major Decision: Which Route Should You Choose to Go with Medicare?

CHAPTER 6: Medicare Mistake #6: Assuming Preexisting Conditions Don't Matter   121

The Problem of too Many Choices   122

Medicare Mistake #6: Assuming Preexisting Conditions Don't Matter   124

The Patient Protection and Affordable Care Act 124

Medicare and Preexisting Conditions 125

Option 1: Original Medicare + Medigap 126

Eligibility for Medicare Supplements (Medigap) 131

Choosing a Medigap Policy 132

Popular Plan Choices 134

Other Medigap Plans 139

Medicare SELECT 140

Nonstandard States: Wisconsin, Minnesota, 141
and Massachusetts

Your "Golden Ticket" to Buying a Medigap Plan 141

Facts about the Open Enrollment Period for Medigap 143

What Happens if You Work Past Age 65? 144

Guaranteed Issue (GI) Periods 145

Exceptions to the One-Time Medigap OEP Rule 147

How Do You Qualify for a Medigap Plan? 149

What Should You Expect from 150
Medigap Underwriting?

Minor Health Conditions—Likely Approval 151

Pending Surgeries and Treatment—Finish Them First 152

Recent Major Care—You'll Need to Wait 153

Chronic Health Conditions—Keep Your 155
Current Coverage

Borderline Health Conditions—Could Go Either Way 155

Auto-Decline Medications and Script Checks 156

A Word about Medical Records 158

Submitting a Medigap Application 158

Key Takeaways 161

CHAPTER 7: Medicare Mistake #7: Canceling Part B because You Joined a Medicare Advantage Plan · 165

Medicare Mistake #7: Canceling Part B because You Joined a Medicare Advantage Plan · 166

Option 2: Medicare Advantage Plans (Part C) · 168

Medicare Advantage Requirements · 172

How Do Medicare Advantage Plans Make Money? · 173

Medicare Advantage Plan Networks · 175

Common Network Types: HMO and PPO · 175

Special Needs Plans · 179

Other Things to Know about Medicare Advantage Plans · 181

Enrollment Periods for Medicare Advantage Plans · 186

Other Medicare Plans · 192

How Do You Choose? · 193

Key Takeaways · 195

CHAPTER 8: Medicare Mistake #8: The Big Mistake · 197

Medicare Mistake #8: Confusing Your One-Time Medigap Open Enrollment Period (Medigap OEP) with the Fall AEP · 198

You Get One Shot at the Medigap OEP · 198

Approval for Medigap Is not always Guaranteed · 199

What Is the Annual Election Period (AEP) For? · 201

Medigap Rate Increases Are not Linked to the Fall AEP · 203

States with Exceptions · 204

What Does not Change During the AEP? · 207

Key Takeaways · 208

Part V—Major Decisions: Which Insurance Plan Should You Select? Should You Stick with It?

CHAPTER 9: Medicare Mistake #9: Asking Your Doctor's Office the Wrong Questions (or not Asking at All) — 213

Doctors and Medicare — 217

How Do You Ask Your Doctors about Plan Participation? — 215

Your Questions Must Be Specific — 216

Check the Plan Directory — 218

A Word about Multiple Doctors — 220

Hard-to-Find Specialties — 220

Narrowing Down Your Choices — 223

What not to Consider — 225

Key Takeaways — 226

CHAPTER 10: Medicare Mistake #10: Annual Decisions—Failing to Review Your Coverage — 229

Medigap Plans – No Annual Change in Core Benefits — 229

Medicare's Rates Go Up each Year — 230

How Do Medigap Companies Set Prices? — 231

How Do Medigap Rate Increases Work? — 234

How and When Should You Shop Your Medigap Plan? — 234

Medicare Advantage Plans and Part D — 235

How Do You Shop Your Medicare Advantage or Part D Policy? — 237

What Changes Can You Make During the Annual Election Period? — 239

What Are some Common Reasons People Change Part D and Medicare Advantage Plans?   240

Key Takeaways   241

CHAPTER 11: Summing Up: A Checklist of the 10 Medicare Mistakes to Avoid (and the 5 Major Decisions You Must Make)   243

What's Not a Mistake—Starting Your Research Early   243

Medicare Is Great Coverage   244

The Major Decisions You'll Face about Medicare   245

10 Medicare Mistakes to Avoid   246

Next Steps   251

CHAPTER 12: Next Steps: More Learning Resources   253

Your Book Bonus   *Tool Kit info*   254

Our Medicare Blog   255

Our Popular "New to Medicare" Webinars   256

6-Day Medicare E-mail Course   256

Learn Medicare with me on YouTube   256

Medicare Q&A with Boomer Benefits (Private Facebook Group)   257

Get Free Help from Our Team   257

The Benefits of Working with an Independent Medicare Agency   258

It's not too Late   258

Federal Government Resources   259

Glossary   261

Acknowledgements   279

Notes   283

Introduction

Are you feeling overwhelmed by all the Medicare information coming your way? If so, you are not alone.

I can picture your desk or kitchen table right now. It's piled high with Medicare brochures, mailers, flyers, leaflets, and postcards. You save them because you aren't sure if you really need them or what you can throw away.

And how about those telemarketers? Is your phone already blowing up with people promising to sell you the right plan?

The problem is you don't even understand how Medicare itself works much less all the supplemental options. With so much information being thrown at you, it's no wonder you might have trouble making sense of it all.

Fortunately, it doesn't have to be this way.

Yes, Medicare is complicated. In fact, I was initially stunned at its complexity when I first began studying it back in 2005. But as I've helped Medicare beneficiaries navigate their entry into Medicare over the last 15 years, I've realized that there are only a few major decisions that you will need to make.

Once you understand how to make these decisions, everything else will fall into place.

What often goes wrong is that people never make them or make wrong decisions that ultimately cost them a lot of money and hassle. But that's not going to happen to you because I'm going to map it all out for you. Here are the **five major deci-sions** that everyone faces when it comes to Medicare:

1. **Major Decision**: When is your **best time** to enroll?
2. **Major Decision**: Will you need **prescription drug coverage**?
3. **Major Decision**: Which of **two routes** should you go with Medicare?
4. **Major Decision**: Which **insurance plan (and company)** should you select?
5. **Major Decision**: Every year: Should you stick with your **current plan or change**?

Within each of these areas, there are certain *big mistakes* that you could potentially make. So, as we go through these decisions, I'll point out WHERE, WHEN, and HOW costly Medicare mistakes happen so that everything will be in context. You will learn where along your personal Medicare journey you need to watch out for them. By the time you have finished reading this book, you will:

- understand the basics of Medicare and how it works;
- have a clear picture of what Medicare covers, and what it doesn't;
- know how to avoid lifelong penalties and preexisting condition limitations by enrolling at the right time and taking advantage of given open enrollment windows; and
- be able to avoid the ten major mistakes (and other pit-falls) that so many people make.

The treasure you will find at the end of this road map is the fantastic feeling you'll get when it all begins to make sense. You'll feel confident in making good decisions in selecting the right coverage for you.

I will also provide you with an amazing book bonus chock full of helpful timelines and checklists that will simplify so much of this. Everyone who buys this book will gain free access to this useful online Medicare toolkit.

My team at Boomer Benefits and I have helped more than 50,000 people make sense of Medicare. In doing so, I've had the opportunity to see just about everything that can (and does) go wrong when it comes to Medicare. I have also learned how to break down this beast of a national health insurance program into a simple decision tree that you can follow. My mission is to make it easier for you to navigate the system—and that's why I've written this book. And before we close here, I want to share with you why I do what I do.

I'll never forget a local engineer who walked into our office here in Fort Worth, Texas, several years ago. He was preparing to retire from Lockheed Martin Aeronautics and looking for guidance about his health coverage in retirement. He came into the conference room, tossed his copy of the 120-page *Medicare and You Handbook* onto the table in front of me, and said, "I'm a relatively smart guy. You could even say that I build fighter jets for a living. But I actually feel dumber after attempting to read this Medicare handbook. None of it makes a lick of sense to me."

It would have been funny except that he wasn't laughing. Sound familiar?

In that moment, looking at his bewildered expression,

I vowed that I would spend my career making this easier for people like him, and you.

So, grab a coffee or your favorite beverage and let's get started!

Part 1

The Basics

Chapter
1

MEDICARE MISTAKE #1:

Assuming that
Medicare Is Free

I've got good news and bad news for you.

The good news is that *part* of Medicare is free for most people when they enroll in Medicare. That's because you've already paid taxes during your working years to cover the cost.

The bad news is that the rest of Medicare is not free, and assuming so is the first mistake that we see many people make when it comes to Medicare.

Medicare Mistake #1: Assuming Medicare Is Free

Assuming Medicare is free can leave you blindsided when you reach age 65. The truth is that Medicare has never been free. It has monthly premiums that you will pay for the rest of your life.

I have met hundreds of people over the years who didn't know Medicare cost anything until the day they enrolled. Many others knew that Medicare has monthly premiums but didn't realize that their incomes would affect how high those premiums might be.

I hope that you are *not* just now learning that Medicare is not free, but even if you are, knowledge is power. Once you learn that Medicare is not free, you can decide whether you have put enough savings away to pay for Medicare in retirement or whether it's important to do some additional earning and saving for future Medicare costs before you retire.

Let's start our Medicare journey together with an overview of what Medicare covers and how much it costs. This overview will give you some background and context for understanding the big decisions you will soon make about Medicare. We won't get into every nitty-gritty detail here. For example, I'm not going to cover Medicare appeals and grievances. You don't need to know about that right now when you've only just begun learning the basics. Instead, we've got great videos to help you with those things down the line, if and when you ever need them.

Some Medicare educators overwhelm their readers with far too much information. upfront—more than you ever need to know just to get started. This paralyzes their readers with inaction. We won't be doing that. However, in this high-level view of Medicare, we'll cover the important basics that set the stage for everything else I'll share with you in this book. That said, Medicare has many big insurance words that can confuse even the brightest person. If you begin to feel confused, stick with me. Things will come together as we go along.

Understanding Medicare Starts with the Parts

When Medicare was created and rolled out back in 1965, legislators had to determine which kinds of services Medicare would cover and which things it would not. Many things made the cut, and a few odd things didn't. Ultimately, they divided Medicare into two parts: inpatient coverage and outpatient coverage. Many years later, they added two additional parts: a private Medicare option and drug coverage.

Each part covers something different, and not everyone needs all four parts.

The first two parts, which have been around since the beginning, are Parts A and B. Together, we call these Original Medicare. They make up the foundation of your healthcare coverage in retirement. You can ONLY get these two parts from the federal government. Everything else, like supplemental coverage, is built upon them, added to your Parts A and B. You enroll in both Parts A and B before you will become eligible to purchase supplemental coverage such as a Medigap plan. By the way, these are also the *only* two parts that you'll sign up for via the Social Security office or the Railroad Retirement Board. If you decide to enroll in Parts C or D, you'll do that through a private insurance company or a broker like Boomer Benefits, but more on that later.

Let's dive into the parts here to see the types of medically necessary care that Medicare provides.

Medicare Part A

Medicare Part A is your inpatient hospital coverage. Think of this as your "room and board" in the hospital. The hospital will provide you with a semiprivate room and meals during your stay. Nurses will care for you during your stay. Part A also covers blood transfusions, hospice care, and skilled-nursing facility stays up to 100 days while you recover from an illness or surgery that put you in the hospital in the first place. In case you were wondering, Medicare Part A provides for *both* medical and mental care. Should you need inpatient mental health care, Medicare Part A will pay as it does for inpatient medical health care *but only for up to a total of 190 days in your lifetime.*

Medicare Part B

In the Medicare 101 webinars that I often teach, I like to say that your Part B outpatient coverage covers pretty much everything else. Most people tend to think of outpatient services as doctor office visits and lab tests. Still, *Part B also pays for other outpatient products and services* like ambulance transportation, medical supplies, durable medical equipment, physical therapy, speech therapy, occupational therapy, mental health care, oxygen, chemotherapy, radiation, and dialysis.

Furthermore, Part B covers essential preventive services, usually at 100 percent, when you receive these services from a doctor who accepts Medicare assignment. (I'll explain assignment later.) Preventive care includes several necessary vaccines, mammograms, colonoscopies, bone mass measurements, and a wide variety of screenings for conditions like diabetes, cardiovascular disease, cancer, depression, alcohol misuse, and obesity, among other things.

It also covers an annual wellness visit, but this visit is fairly limited in scope. Medicare's wellness visits are not as thorough as the kind of annual physicals you may have had in the past using your employer or individual health coverage. Once your coverage is set up, you'll want to spend some time learning about preventive care services, what they cover, and how often they are covered. (You can find more about this in our learning resources provided at the end of this book.)

Certain types of medications also fall under Medicare Part B instead of Part D. Part B drugs are generally drugs that a doctor or other medical professional administers to you in a clinical or hospital setting. Examples of Part B drugs are intravenous chemotherapy medications or medications delivered via a piece of durable medical equipment such as insulin pumps or nebulizers (for breathing medications). Part B also covers diabetic supplies like lancets, test strips, and glucose monitors. Most of these medications or items are costly, and you wouldn't want to pay for them out-of-pocket.

There is one last point I want to make about Part B. Occasionally, we run across people who never enrolled in Part B because they considered themselves "healthy" and decided to go without outpatient coverage. This can put you in a world of hurt if you end up needing ambulatory surgery or cancer treatment and have no coverage to pay for it. If Medicare will be your primary coverage, then both Medicare Parts A and B are vital.

FAQ: Does Medicare have a maximum out-of-pocket limit on what it will cover?

ANSWER: There is not a dollar limit to what Medicare will cover for medically necessary services. There are some services where Medicare has a maximum number of consecutive days allowed though, such as for inpatient hospital benefits, which we'll discuss. There are also other services where Medicare may decide you've exceeded what is reasonable in one calendar year, such as physical therapy. For the most part, however, Medicare will provide as much medically necessary care as is needed. You will pay your share of the cost of some of these services though, as I'll explain shortly.

Okay, so we've covered Original Medicare Parts A and B. Now, let's look at the other two parts, which came later.

4 PARTS OF MEDICARE

PART A	PART B	PART C	PART D
Hospital Insurance	Medical Insurance	Medicare Advantage Plans	Prescription Drug Plans

Figure 1-1.

Medicare Part C

Part C is the optional Medicare Advantage program. Our legislators created it as part of the Balanced Budget Act of 1997. It gives Medicare beneficiaries like you an option to get your Parts A and B health-care services through a private insurance company instead of through Medicare itself. Since I'll cover Medicare Advantage plans in-depth in a later chapter, let's move on to Part D.

Medicare Part D

Medicare Part D is an optional program to help you pay for outpatient prescriptions. It is also the newest part of Medicare. I can't even begin to tell you how happy I was when our federal government rolled it out in 2006. For nearly half a century before that, beneficiaries did not have adequate coverage for outpatient prescription medicines. We are very fortunate to have it today. Imagine being diabetic and having to pay 100 percent of the cost of expensive insulin. Many people found themselves in this situation before Part D came along. We sometimes had clients who spent more than $10K per year on their diabetes medications back then. It's no coincidence that more than 70 percent of beneficiaries[1] participate in the Part D program today.

Although the Part D program is far better than what we had before, which was nothing, Part D isn't perfect. It doesn't cover 100 percent of your drug costs. You will pay your share of the cost of your medications. There's a penalty that may also apply if you don't enroll in Part D, which we'll cover in detail later.

Part D plans also change their benefits annually, which is why so many beneficiaries find Part D to be the most confusing part of Medicare. You'll need to research your options each fall, but I'm going to show you how to use free resources to help you with this, such as your personal portal at MyMedicare.gov. (In chapter 4, we'll take a deeper dive into how Medicare Part D works and why this coverage is so important.)

Medicare Is Far from Free

The various parts of Medicare all have costs associated with them. Yet for some reason, the myth that Medicare is free or nearly free persists. Some new beneficiaries assume that not only will Medicare be free but also expect that Medicare will cover healthcare costs in retirement in total. In other words, they think that it will cover 100 percent of all their medical-care expenses for the rest of their lives.

Consider Deborah, who e-mailed me after attending one of our New to Medicare webinars. Deborah's e-mail was like dozens of other e-mails we receive each year from new Medicare beneficiaries who are just finding this out. However, her message was perhaps a little more colorful.

In her e-mail, she expressed her outrage about the federal government charging "unsuspecting" citizens for Medicare. She was preparing to retire soon. Like any well-prepared person, she had been researching her Social Security and Medicare options. She didn't get very far before she came across what she called "a huge problem." Deborah shared with us that she was "shocked, appalled, and dismayed" to discover that the "thieving federal government was hoodwinking the American public."

How so?

By allowing people to believe their payroll deductions throughout their working lives "actually paid for their health care someday."

While she was particularly colorful in her choice of words, Deborah is undoubtedly not alone. Every month we meet dozens of new beneficiaries approaching age 65 with absolutely no idea that Medicare isn't free.

It's not hard to understand why.

Most Americans know vaguely that Medicare and Social Security are out there waiting for them when the time finally comes to retire. In fact, throughout their entire working lives, most American workers see deductions for these two programs on their paychecks that look like this:

Taxes	Current	YTD Amount
Medicare Employee Addl Tax	0.00	0.00
Federal Withholding	-124.00	-4,736.00
Social Security Employee	-96.78	-3,508.75
Medicare Employee	-22.63	-820.59
	-243.41	-9,065.34

Figure 1-2. Common Payroll Deductions.

It's not difficult to see why that would be misleading, but it's also hugely problematic when you learn this too late. Many people like Deborah are entirely unprepared to spend 10–20 percent or more of their Social Security retirement income on their Medicare Parts B and D coverage.

And that's not all you'll spend, either.

Medicare has cost-sharing expenses that you'll pay out of your pocket as you use your health-care benefits, just like there is now when you use your under-65 health-care benefits from your employer or individual health plan. You pay your share of the costs in the form of deductibles, coinsurance, and copays. You'll do the same with Medicare.

Then there is also the cost of either a Medigap or Medicare Advantage plan to help you cover some of the things that otherwise you would pay out-of-pocket if Medicare is your only coverage. If you prefer not to worry about what sort of medical bills will show up in your mailbox after an illness or hospital stay, you'll want to consider enrolling in a Medigap plan or Medicare Advantage plan.

When you add all these costs together, you'll soon find out that Medicare is likely to cost you thousands of dollars per year. The Kaiser Family Foundation released a study in 2018[2] showing that Medicare beneficiaries' average out-of-pocket spending toward health-care costs was equal to 41 percent of their average Social Security income. Considering that tens of millions of retirees count on Social Security for more than 90 percent of their income, these unexpected Medicare premiums can be very upsetting if you don't find out anything about them until you are ready to retire.

So, what exactly do those payroll deductions pay for? What can you personally expect to pay when you finally age into Medicare? I'll explain this next and show you how you can begin to estimate these future costs for yourself.

To help you, we've created a Medicare costs worksheet, which you can find inside our *Medicare Toolkit* on the special book bonus site that we've created for everyone who has purchased this book. You can record your estimated costs for Medicare Parts A, B, and D as we go along. Find out how to access the toolkit in Chapter 12.

Medicare Costs AND Cost-Sharing Expenses

There are two kinds of expenses you'll pay when you have Medicare. These are:

1. The cost of the insurance itself, which we call the monthly premiums; and
2. Cost-sharing expenses that you'll pay at the time you receive medical services.

Here in America, we are used to paying our share of the health care that we receive before we turn 65, and that doesn't change when you enroll in Medicare.

I want you to think about your current health insurance, which your employer or spouse's employer probably provided to you. However, it might also be a policy you purchased through the Affordable Care Act (ACA) marketplace if your employer doesn't provide health benefits or if you are self-employed.

Is your current pre-65 health insurance coverage entirely free for you?

Probably not.

And when you use the medical services under that plan, does it pay for 100 percent of your medical expenses?

No, it probably doesn't.

Instead, you've shared in both of these types of costs over the years. Your employer deducts your portion of the cost of that health insurance out of your payroll. Those are your *monthly health insurance premiums*. Likewise, when you visited the doctor, you likely paid a copay to do so. If you need to stay in a hospital, you also know that you will pay the deductible before the insurance kicks in. These things are your *cost-sharing expenses*.

I'm pointing this out because Medicare works similarly to your under-65 health insurance in that it has both premiums that you pay for the coverage and cost-sharing expenses that you pay as you seek health services. And yet, so many people assume that when they sign up for Medicare, everything will be free, and they won't spend a dime on their health care. That is not the case, and now that you know that, we can begin preparing you for what each of those costs will be.

Let's start with the monthly Medicare premiums. A **premium** is the amount of money that you pay for the insurance coverage itself. In this case, that insurance coverage comes from Medicare. Still, it works the same way as monthly premiums that you might pay to an auto insurance company. For example, you give the auto insurance company a monthly sum of money. In return, they take on the risk that you might have a car accident. Medicare is the same. With Medicare, you'll pay a monthly premium to the federal government because they agree to take on your risk of health spending for an illness or injury.

Your Premiums for Medicare Part A

Here's some excellent news: Chances are good that you will pay nothing for Part A at the time of your enrollment.

Remember those Medicare payroll deductions that they withdrew from your paychecks all those years? Those deductions go into the Medicare program to pay for workers' future Part A hospital benefits. The Federal Insurance Contributions Act (FICA) of 1935 created a system in which workers make mandatory contributions to Social Security out of every paycheck during their working years. Later, when President Johnson signed Medicare into law in 1965, Congress added a similar contribution from employees' payroll checks to fund Medicare, too. If you (or your spouse) have paid these FICA taxes for at least 40 quarters (or 10 years) in your lifetime, Part A will cost you nothing. (Self-employed individuals pay these FICA taxes, too, so if you worked for yourself over the years, you should have accumulated plenty of quarters.)

How Do Workers Pay for Part A?

To pay for your future Part A hospital coverage, Uncle Sam

taxes employees like you at a rate of 1.45 percent of all your income. Your employer contributes the same percentage as you do toward these future benefits, so both you and your employers help fund the Medicare program.

The Affordable Care Act also added an extra tax for high-income earners, called the Additional Medicare Tax. Individual employees who earn more than $200,000 and joint filers who earn more than $250,000 pay an additional 0.9 percent in Medicare taxes beyond the regular 1.45 percent. Taken together, this is no small chunk of change.

So, if you or your spouse have worked the necessary 40 quarters in the United States and paid FICA taxes during those years, you will pay nothing for Part A once you are enrolled. *Your Part A premiums at that point are zero.* Coincidentally, this is the same number (40) of quarters that you need to qualify for Social Security retirement benefits. Anyone with those earnings can expect to pay nothing for Part A once they are using it.

What If You Don't Have Enough Quarters?

Most Medicare beneficiaries qualify for premium-free Part A, but some beneficiaries must pay for Part A. The most common example is immigrants who haven't lived in the United States long enough to pay in the necessary quarters. Also, some federal or state workers may not pay FICA taxes. These Medicare beneficiaries can still get premium-free Part A if their spouse is eligible for Social Security benefits and has worked the necessary quarters. They must have been married for at least a year. Likewise, if they have a former spouse who is eligible for Social Security benefits, and they were married to that spouse for at least ten years, they can qualify for premium-free Part A through their ex-spouse.

If none of the above applies to you, then you can buy a health insurance plan through the federal exchange at age 65, or you can purchase Part A. Either way, it doesn't come cheap. Purchasing Medicare Part A in 2021 will cost you around $471/month. However, people with less than 40 quarters of work experience but more than 30 quarters can get a prorated premium of $259/month. To buy Part A, you must have been a citizen, legal resident, or have had a green card for at least five years. Considering that Medicare Part A covers up to 150 consecutive days in the hospital and other benefits like skilled-nursing care and hospice care, it's not a bad deal even at that price. It's just that many Americans don't realize that their FICA taxes *only* go toward prepaying Part A.

Your Premiums for Medicare Part B

So far, so good, right? Most of you will pay nothing for Part A once you enroll.

Part B, however, is a different story. Here we come to the part of Medicare that irked Deborah so much. *While your payroll taxes during your working years pay for Part A, they do not pay for Part B. Medicare beneficiaries pay a monthly premium for Part B for as long as they are enrolled in it, which is generally for the rest of their lives.* The base premium for Medicare Part B in 2021 is $148.50 per month. Medicare determines this premium and tends to increase it a bit each year. Part B is a per-person cost, so if you are married, you will each pay your own Part B premium.

Social Security will deduct your monthly Part B premiums from your Social Security checks once you enroll in retirement benefits. If you have not enrolled in Social Security retirement benefits, then they'll bill you. You can also sign up for Medicare Easy Pay, a free service that will automatically deduct your premiums monthly from your savings or checking account.

Unfortunately, many workers are never aware of these future Part B premiums. They are naturally upset to learn of this upon retirement, especially when the average Social Security check for retired workers is only around $1,514/month[3]. While most people pay the standard base premium for Part B, some people will pay considerably more than that (as I explain in the following section). Learning about this too late could be disastrous for your retirement plans.

Let's look at how this works.

The Income-Related Monthly Adjustment Amount (IRMAA)

The Social Security office determines your Medicare Part B premiums based upon your modified, adjusted, gross income (MAGI).

To determine your personal Part B premium, the Social Security office will pull your IRS tax return from two years ago. They'll use that tax return to determine whether you will owe an Income-Related Monthly Adjustment Amount on top of the base Part B premium. (Part D premiums are also affected by your income, which we'll discuss shortly.)

For example, in 2021, Social Security will calculate your Parts B and D premiums based on your 2019 income. Individuals earning more than $88,000 filing individually or $176,000 filing jointly can expect to pay more than the standard base Part B premium. The items that contribute to your MAGI include things like money earned through wages, interest, required minimum distributions from investments, and capital gains. It also includes Social Security benefits and tax-deferred pensions.

Distributions from Roth IRAs and Roth 401(k)s, life insurance, reverse mortgages, and health savings accounts do *not* count in the MAGI calculation. For more on what does and doesn't count in calculating your premiums, visit this page: https://boomerbenefits.com/new-to-medicare/medicare-cost/.

MEDICARE 2021 PART B PREMIUMS
IF YOUR FILING STATUS AND YEARLY INCOME IN 2019 WAS:

FILE INDIVIDUAL TAX RETURN	FILE JOINT TAX RETURN	MARRIED & SEPARATE TAX RETURN	IN 2021 YOU WILL PAY
$88k or less	$176k or less	$88k or less	$148.50/month
$88k+ to $111k	$176k+ to $222k	N/A	$207.90/month
$111k+ to $138k	$222k+ to $276k	N/A	$297.00/month
$138k+ to $165k	$276k+ to $330k	N/A	$386.10/month
$165k+ to $499.9k	$330k+ to $749.9k	$88k+ to $411.9k	$475.20/month
$500k+	$750k+	$412k+	$504.90/month

each $2↑

Figure 1-3.

> Dave and Sue are married and file their taxes jointly. They had a modified, adjusted, gross income in 2019 of $250,000. Social Security will assess EACH of their individual Medicare premiums in 2021 at $297. Dave and Sue will each pay a separate monthly premium of $297/month, and that's before adding on Medigap or Part D coverage.

If you file your taxes jointly with a spouse, Social Security will base your premiums on your joint income. However, you will EACH pay your own Part B premium. Your premiums for

Part B are always individual, never combined. Social Security simply uses your household income to determine what each of you will pay for Part B.

Let's look at an example: John and Mary earned a combined income of $200,000 in 2019. John will pay $2,027.90 for his Part B in 2021. Mary will also pay the same for her Part B. Because your income often changes from year to year, Social Security will review this information annually. They usually notify you by mail of your next year's premium each year in December or early January.

The Kaiser Family Foundation reported that in 2017 only about 6.6 percent[4] of beneficiaries enrolled in Part B pay higher Medicare premiums. However, some of them surely didn't know about the higher price tag ahead of time. You can bet that you would feel distressed if you learned of the IRMAA after you had already been planning that Part B would cost you only the base amount. For instance, selling property or stock or receiving an inheritance could affect your Medicare Parts B and D premiums that are based on that tax year. I've seen a fair number of people decide to delay retirement for a few extra years when they were surprised by an IRMAA that made Part B much more expensive than anticipated.

BOOMER BENEFITS PRO TIP: Most people earn more annually while working than they do when they retire. Suppose your income was higher two years ago than it is today because you have now retired, and your Medicare premiums are based on that higher income.

You can file an appeal to lower your premiums with Social Security. Other life-changing events that affect your income such as marriage or divorce could also help you win an appeal to lower your premiums. It's relatively easy to file this appeal, and we've got a blog post (and YouTube video) to help you through that, both of which you can find here: https://boomerbenefits.com/reconsideration/

Now that we've covered what you'll spend for Original Medicare Parts A and B benefits, let's talk about the rest, which are optional parts.

Your Premiums for Medicare Parts C and D

Medicare Part C and Part D are voluntary programs. It is essential that you understand them both so you can decide whether you wish to participate in them.

Part C is the Medicare Advantage program. If you decide to enroll in Part C, you will pay the monthly premium set by the plan. (In some cases, the plan may charge no monthly premium.) These premiums vary by plan, so we'll discuss costs for these plans in the upcoming chapter about your choices between Medigap plans and Medicare Advantage plans.

Part D is the Medicare Prescription Drug program. Many beneficiaries do enroll in Part D coverage because there are late penalties if you fail to enroll when you are first eligible unless you have other creditable drug coverage. Unlike Medicare Parts A and B, you don't sign up for Part D through the Social Security office. Instead, private insurance companies offer Part D drug plans. In some cases, Part D is included in a Medicare Advantage plan and at no extra price. Your base premium for Part D will vary depending on which plan you choose.

There is a wide range of Part D plans in every state. The average monthly premiums for the 21 national standalone Part D plans range from around $7/month on the low end to around $89/month on the high end.[5] Though all plans must include certain medications mandated by Medicare, plans with higher premiums often have richer drug formularies and coverage. (**A formulary** is a list of prescription drugs offered by a specific Part D insurance plan.)

The national *average* premium for a standalone Part D drug plan is approximately $41/month.[6] This is a good number to plug into your planning worksheet if you are working on estimating your future costs. You should also know that if you are a high-income earner, that high income can affect Part D just like it affects Part B premiums with an income-related adjustment.

If the Social Security office calculates that you owe an IRMAA, they will bill you separately; they will use the same form of payment method you have chosen to use to pay the ordinary Part D plan premium. Social Security bills your Part D IRMAA along with your Part B IRMAA. You pay that directly to Medicare, not to the Part D company.

If you aren't yet taking Social Security income benefits from which they can deduct your Medicare premiums, Social Security will bill you for both the regular Part B premiums and the IRMAAs that you owe. The IRMAA bills come separately from your regular Part B quarterly invoice the first time it is ever assessed. This confuses many people. They don't understand why they got two separate invoices, and sometimes they fail to pay the second one. *Don't miss paying either of these invoices. Failure to pay your IRMAA bills can result in cancellation of both your Part B benefits and your Part D policy.*

MEDICARE 2021 PART D PREMIUMS
IF YOUR FILING STATUS AND YEARLY INCOME IN 2019 WAS:

FILE INDIVIDUAL TAX RETURN	FILE JOINT TAX RETURN	MARRIED & SEPARATE TAX RETURN	IN 2021 YOU WILL PAY
$88k or less	$176k or less	$88k or less	Your plan premium
$88k+ to $111k	$176k+ to $222k	N/A	$12.30 + your plan premium
$111k+ to $138k	$222k+ to $276k	N/A	$31.80 + your plan premium
$138k+ to $165k	$276k+ to $330k	N/A	$51.20 + your plan premium
$165k+ to $499.9k	$330k+ to $749.9k	$88k+ to $411.9k	$70.70 + your plan premium
$500k+	$750k+	$412k+	$77.10 + your plan premium

Figure 1-4.

Since Part D is voluntary, a Part D IRMAA that increases your cost may affect your decision to enroll in Part D. This is a personal decision. Someone with a very high income who takes little to no medication may determine that the expense isn't worth it.

However, I recommend that you consider enrolling in at least the cheapest plan in your state to avoid late penalties, which are cumulative and ongoing. You also want to have coverage on hand when you experience an illness that requires expensive medication. I'll give you some examples in a later chapter about the catastrophic spending I've seen several beneficiaries go through when they decided to skip Part D.

Key Takeaways

We've learned a lot in this chapter, including that:

- Medicare is not free and does not cover 100% of your health care costs.
- Part A is your hospital coverage.
- Part B is your outpatient coverage.
- Part C is the optional Medicare Advantage program.
- Part D is the optional federal program to help pay for outpatient prescriptions.
- The various parts of Medicare all have costs associated with them.

Let's also take a minute to recap what you have learned about the premiums and cost-sharing you will pay:

- Medicare Part A costs $0 for most people, but premiums are paid for Parts B and D.
- Most beneficiaries pay $148.50 per month for just Part B but some pay more based on their income.
- Part D premiums vary, but in most states, you can find plans starting around $7/month.
- This is an approximate total of at least $156/month for Medicare Parts A, B, and D (more for people with higher incomes).
- This is *before* you pay for supplemental coverage that will help to cover your share of the costs of medical services, which we'll cover in the next chapter.

Are you still with me?

You may find it challenging to get your head around

everything that Medicare covers and costs but stay with me. It will begin to make more sense as we go along. I'll also give you some additional "Learning Resources" in Chapter 12 that will help things come together for you.

I often wish Medicare offered a class for people at age 50 to give them some warning about their potential spending on Medicare. It would certainly help people who are diligently saving for their financial futures but have not considered the costs of health care in that future. Instead, they mistakenly think they will pay nothing for Medicare. Since that class doesn't exist to prepare you for the costs of Medicare, I'm outlining them for you here.

If you have a question about the basics we've covered here or about anything else we cover in the upcoming chapters, you can join me in our free private Facebook group where we can answer questions for beneficiaries like you. You can find that here: https://boomerbenefits.link/Medicare-Questions

Okay, so we have covered your Medicare upfront costs (premiums). That's one part of the costs you'll incur for Medicare. Now let's discuss that second part—your cost-sharing expenses, or what you will pay over the years as you use various medical services.

Chapter 2

MEDICARE MISTAKE #2:

Expecting Medicare to Cover 100% of Your Medical Costs

In the last chapter, I shared that Medicare has two types of costs. I explained that the first part involved your monthly premiums. However, paying those premiums doesn't mean Medicare then covers every penny of your medical services. You will still have the same kinds of cost-sharing expenses at the time of treatment that you have now with your under-65 health coverage.

Medicare Mistake #2: Expecting that Medicare Will Cover 100% of Your Medical Costs

Medicare has deductibles, copays, and coinsurance that you will pay as you use medical services. For example, Medicare Part B covers only 80% of your outpatient health-care costs.

You are responsible for the rest.

While paying 20% of the cost of a doctor visit might not hurt too much, imagine paying 20% of the cost of a knee replacement or an open-heart surgery. And that's not all. You will also be responsible for covering things that fall outside of Medicare but are still health-care related, like dental, vision, hearing, and long-term-care costs. Thousands of people are surprised every year to learn that Original Medicare doesn't cover routine dental and vision services.

So why do some people believe that Medicare will cover everything? Maybe it's because Medicare is a national health insurance program, and Americans think it works like the single-payer system in Canada or Britain.

It doesn't.

In any event, you now know the truth and can plan accordingly. In the upcoming chapters, I'll show you the supplemental options you have for helping to cover deductibles, copays, and that other 20% of your outpatient expenses.

Common Terms

I want to define a few insurance terms that you will see here in case some of the words I'm using are only vaguely familiar.

Health insurance has a language all its own, and Medicare is no exception. (There is also a "Glossary" at the end of the book.)

A Medicare *deductible*, what's that? And how is it different from a Medicare *copay*?

Most of these insurance terms define your out-of-pocket costs. Understanding them will help you learn what you can expect to pay (or have your supplemental coverage pay for you).

*A **deductible** is the amount of money you will pay out of your pocket before your benefits kick in. It is money you pay upfront upon your first covered medical service of the year.*

Using our same car insurance example, think about your deductible on your automobile policy. Suppose you have a $500 deductible on that policy. In the event of an accident, you would pay the first $500 out-of-pocket before the insurance company starts paying anything toward your repairs.

Parts A and B each have a deductible. You will pay this deductible before Medicare begins paying its share of your covered expenses. Medicare itself sets these deductibles, and they usually go up a little bit from year to year. (Part D also has a deductible set by Medicare each year. However, the insurance companies who offer Part D plans can choose whether to charge that full deductible or to reduce it, which we'll cover in Chapter 4.)

*A **copay or coinsurance** is your share of a covered health-care expense after you have met the deductible.* A copay is often a fixed-dollar amount. You are probably already familiar with paying flat copays when you visit the doctor or fill a prescription. Coinsurance, on the other hand, is usually expressed as a percentage but can sometimes be a fixed-dollar amount as well. Think about the 80/20 health insurance coverage your employer has likely provided you with in the past. After you had met your deductible for the year, the employer insurance may have paid 80%, and you paid 20%. That 20% is called your coinsurance.

As we move into discussing your Medicare costs, you can refer back to these definitions or the "Glossary" for help understanding the terminology.

Also, please know that anytime you read the words **Medigap plan, that means the same thing as a Medicare supplement**, which is an insurance policy that we'll cover later in the book.

So *Medigap plan = Medicare supplement*. Two different terms, but both refer to the same kind of policy. In this book, I'll mostly use the term *Medigap plan* to keep things simple. Now let's get back to discussing your share of health-care services.

Medicare Cost-Sharing Expenses: What Do You Pay for as You Go?

Preparing for the costs that you'll pay as you obtain covered Medicare services is one of the most critical things any retiree can do. You would never want expenses like these to sneak up on you unexpectedly, so I am going to walk you through them. There may come a moment where you feel bewildered and wonder why Medicare made it all so complicated. The good news is that you don't have to memorize any of this. I'm sharing these costs with you here so that you can see what your expenses would be with just Medicare alone. However, I'll show you later how you can cover almost all of these costs with a supplemental policy.

Your Part A Cost-Sharing Expenses

The tricky part about Part A is that your cost-sharing expenses are based on benefit periods, not calendar years. Medicare defines a *benefit period* as the way that Original Medicare measures your use of inpatient hospital and skilled nursing facility (SNF) care.

A benefit period begins the day you are admitted to the hospital or to SNF. It ends when you have left the hospital and go 60 consecutive days without any covered inpatient hospital or SNF care.

FAQ: How many Part A benefit periods am I allowed in my lifetime?

Answer: There is no limit to the number of benefit periods.

I will further explain and clarify benefit periods in the next few sections. But let's look at how they affect your hospital spending.

Part A Deductible

Part A, your inpatient hospital coverage, requires a deductible that you will pay for inpatient care and other Part A services when you are admitted as an inpatient.

In 2021, the Part A deductible is $1,484 per benefit period. During each benefit period, Medicare will cover up to 90 days of inpatient hospitalization before you begin using lifetime reserve days (more on those reserve days later). The Part A deductible applies to each "benefit period" in which you receive covered Part A services. You could potentially have several different benefit periods in a single year if you were going in and out of the hospital. In other words, it's possible to pay the Part A deductible *more than once per year*.

BENEFITS PERIOD EXAMPLE

Below is an example of a benefit period, which closes 60 days after the discharge date. If you are readmitted before the benefit period closes, you generally do not pay the deductible again.

Admitted on April 1	Discharged on April 10	Benefit period ends June 9
DAY 1	**DAY 10**	**60 DAYS LATER**

Figure 2-1

Here's an example of how this might look in real life (see figure 2-1). Let's say you were admitted to the hospital on April 1 and got discharged on April 10. Your benefit period would begin on April 1, the day you entered the hospital. It would end on June 9—60 days after the hospital discharged you.

Medicare will apply the deductible to the first invoices received from your hospital or SNF. This means Medicare will "short-pay" that invoice by the amount of your deductible. When the hospital processes that payment, it will send you a bill for the Part A deductible for this benefit period. That's how you pay the deductible.

Now, let's look at the date that closes the benefit period. In this example, the benefit period is scheduled to close on June 9, 60 days after your discharge. If you fall ill again and are readmitted to the hospital before June 9, you would still be within the original benefit period. Therefore, you would *not* have to pay the Part A deductible again for that admission because it occurred within 60 days of your discharge on April 10. The hospital readmitted you *before* the original benefit period had closed.

However, if you were readmitted to the hospital again on June 15, your original benefit period would have already closed on June 9. Now you would start a *new* benefit period, which means you'll pay the Part A deductible again. *Anytime more than 60 days pass between your hospital discharge date and a new hospital or SNF admission, you start a new benefit period and pay a new deductible.*

Understanding benefit periods is a little tricky. If you feel lost, the main takeaway here is this: *It is possible to pay the Part A hospital deductible more than once per year.* It is a hefty pill to swallow for many people who are living on a fixed income. However, I'm going to show you later in this book how you can arrange supplemental coverage that will take care of that Part A deductible for you.

The good news is that your Part A deductible is the only inpatient hospital expense you will pay if your inpatient stay is less than (or up to) 60 days. This next part doesn't affect very many people, but you do need to know about it.

Part A Coinsurance Costs

If you stay in the hospital *longer than 60 days*, Part A also has coinsurance that *you* will pay for covered services received after a certain number of days.

In 2021, *your* Part A coinsurance costs are:

- $0 for days 1–60
- $371 per day for days 61 through 90 in the hospital
- $742 per day from day 91 until 150
- **All** costs after Day 150

Days 91-150 are considered your *lifetime reserve days.* Lifetime reserve days are a bank of 60 inpatient care days that you can use only once during your lifetime. Earlier I explained that during each benefit period, Medicare will cover up to 90 days of inpatient care. After that 90 days, if you are still in the hospital, Medicare will begin drawing from your 60 lifetime reserve days. *After you use those lifetime reserve days, you will pay the full cost of your inpatient care for the rest of your stay.* (However, if you use only some of those lifetime reserve days, the rest are still available to you in the future).

Again, these giant daily copays only affect you in the event of an unusually long hospital stay. Usually, you would leave the hospital before then. However, these are some pretty big numbers that can add up quickly if you are unlucky enough to need inpatient care for more than 90 straight days. Just ten days in the hospital from Day 91-100 would cost you over $7,400!

There's another type of inpatient stay that can also cost you a pretty penny. Sometimes, after you leave the hospital, your doctor will transfer you to a Skilled-Nursing Facility (SNF) to continue your recovery. Just as you pay your share toward hospital costs, you will also share in the expense of your SNF stay.

For example, if after your hospital stay, you need to recover in a facility where skilled nursing is provided, you will pay:

- First 20 days: $0
- Days 21–100: $185.50 per day.
- After Day 100: You pay all costs.

If you stayed in there the whole 100 days, you would pay around $14K.

To qualify for a Medicare-covered SNF stay, you must first have an inpatient hospital stay of 3 days or longer. Your doctor must order the SNF stay for you. You can't just elect to go on your own if you want Medicare to cover it.

Why is that important?

Sometimes, hospitals don't formally admit you into the hospital. Instead, they put you into an "under observation" status. If you aren't officially admitted into the hospital, then you don't qualify for SNF coverage even if you were in the hospital for three days. You could rack up charges without even knowing it. Ask questions to confirm that you qualify for this facility coverage before moving into any SNF for posthospital care.

I realize that some of these numbers start to look big and can be frightening to many people. Remember that extended hospital stays are not that common. We often have people also express concern about those lifetime reserve days, and with good reason. After you have exhausted your lifetime reserve days, you pay ALL hospital costs for the rest of that stay.

This is where supplemental coverage, like a Medigap plan, comes into play. Most supplemental coverage will provide you with 365 additional days of hospital coverage beyond your lifetime reserve days. Then, if you DO have a lengthy hospital stay, you won't worry about paying any daily copays. Many of these plans also pay for your Part A coinsurance—those expensive daily hospital and SNF copays that I showed you earlier. This is important so that you aren't sitting in the hospital worrying over what bills will show up in your mailbox when you get home.

I've now shown you some of the costs related to Part A. Part B has cost-sharing expenses as well, so let's look at that next.

Your Part B Cost-Sharing Expenses

Medicare Part B also has a deductible and coinsurance costs that are your responsibility.

Part B Deductible

In 2021, the Medicare Part B deductible is $203. Unlike the Part A deductible, the Part B deductible is for the calendar year.

You must meet your Medicare Part B deductible only once in each calendar year. Whenever you have your first outpatient health-care services of a calendar year, you'll pay $203 before your benefits kick in.

Let's look at an example, with numbers: Sue's first doctor visit of the year is on January 27. She has a lingering cough after a viral illness and just can't seem to kick the bug. Her doctor tests for strep and then sends her for some additional lab tests down the road at a lab facility the same day. This results in $250 in outpatient charges. Medicare won't pay the first $203 because Sue is responsible for that amount as her Part B deductible. When Medicare processes the claim, it designates that Sue must pay the first $203, and then proceeds to pay its 80% share of the remaining $47.

When Sue's doctor's office receives Medicare's payment, it will apply Medicare's payment toward her account and send Sue a bill for any money that she owes for her deductible and coinsurance. Thus, Sue's invoice will be for her deductible plus her coinsurance (20% of $47 or $9.40, for a total of $212.40). Now Sue is done with her Part B deductible for the rest of the year. However, she will still have to continue to pay coinsurance costs on future medical services.

Remember that car insurance example? If you have a $500 deductible on your auto insurance plan, it means that you will pay the first $500 in out-of-pocket repair costs in the event of an accident. Your insurance policy won't begin to pay its share until you have first satisfied that deductible.

Your Part B deductible works the same way. Sometimes, it may take you a couple of doctor appointments to satisfy it, but rest assured that Medicare is keeping a tally on what you spend.

Once Medicare calculates that you have met the deductible, it will begin to kick in its share of 80%, while you cover the other 20%. This is called your Part B coinsurance.

Part B Coinsurance Costs

Part B covers a whole host of preventive care services at 100%, such as annual wellness visits, mammograms, colonoscopies, and so on. These are great benefits, and you should take full advantage of them.

For everything else, Part B typically pays 80% of the allowable covered charges, and you pay 20%.

I'm sure you will agree that paying 20% of the cost of a doctor visit isn't fun, but it probably won't bankrupt you. However, paying 20% of the expense of six weeks of chemotherapy is a different story altogether. And here's the worst part: There is also no cap on your 20% coinsurance—no stop-loss or out-of-pocket limit to the amount you might spend.

You pay that 20% forever.

This potential risk of paying 20% coinsurance with no cap is one of the biggest reasons that many beneficiaries purchase supplemental coverage. We recently had a caller to our agency who never purchased supplemental coverage. He had only enrolled in Medicare Parts A and B. He had a heart attack and then an open-heart surgery, lots of follow-up care, and cardiac rehab therapy. It cost him thousands of dollars because he was shelling out 20% of most of that care.

Part B "Excess Charges"

We should also mention here that Medicare always pays 80% *of the allowable assignment charges.* New Medicare beneficiaries often don't know what that means, so here's what you need to know.

Medicare decides what it will pay for various types of medical services. They call this the "assigned rates" or "allowable charges." Most health-care providers agree to accept Medicare's assigned rates as payment in full. However, some providers choose not to accept these assigned rates because they feel they are too low. These providers can choose to be a "nonparticipating" Medicare provider, which means they can "balance-bill" you up to an additional 15% beyond what Medicare pays them for seeing you. Medicare refers to this as a Part B "excess charge."

As you can imagine, you may consider it quite a hassle to have to ask each provider if he or she accepts Medicare assignment so that you can avoid paying excess charges. Fortunately, there are specific Medigap plans that will cover these for you.

> **BOOMER BENEFITS PRO TIP:** One last thing I'd like to share on Part B costs. If you age into Medicare late in the year, such as October or November, you'll owe the Part B deductible for any services for that current year (on or before December 31). Then when the new year begins, you'll have a new deductible to satisfy. If you can postpone any doctor appointments or other Part B services until January, you'll save yourself from paying that deductible twice.

Your Part D Cost-Sharing Expenses

I could write an entire book just on how Part D works. The cost-sharing here is more complicated. I don't want to overwhelm you when you've already taken in so much information in this basics chapter. We'll tackle Part D costs in Chapter 4.

What Expenses Does Medicare *not* Cover?

Now that you know what Medicare covers and what your share of the costs for those services are, let's take a moment to discuss a few things that Medicare doesn't cover. These are things that you will need to pay for yourself. Some of them come as quite a surprise to new Medicare beneficiaries. You want to know about them upfront rather than after you've had an expensive procedure only to find that it's not covered. Some of them will seem rather obvious, such as care received outside the United States and cosmetic procedures. Others are less so, such as routine foot care, massage therapy, and other holistic health services. For this section, let's concentrate on the biggies.

Routine Dental, Vision, and Hearing Coverage

It might seem odd that Medicare would choose not to cover routine dental, vision, and hearing services. After all, your later years are precisely the time that you most need coverage for these items. However, when Medicare was drafted into law back in the 1960s, dental, vision, and hearing services were not commonly part of the benefit plans covered by employers like they are today. People didn't expect this coverage in the way that they do now. Moreover, people also didn't live as long in 1965 as they do today, so fewer people had age-related hearing loss. Hearing aids weren't as much of a concern as today when beneficiaries often live into their 80s, 90s, and beyond.

The Medicare Act excluded hearing aids because they were considered low in cost back then and best left to consumers to provide for themselves. It's also fair to say that at the time, the medical community didn't have a great understanding of how things like hearing loss and vision loss can lead to social isolation and, therefore, potentially serious health conditions like depression. Similarly, we know much more today about how the lack of adequate dental care can affect overall health. Legislators in 1965 weren't privy to this information. It is ironic that Medicare's failure to cover preventive dental care probably contributes to some health conditions that it must cover as a result. The Kaiser Family Foundation reported in a press release in early 2019 that 65% of Medicare beneficiaries —or nearly 37 million people—don't have any dental coverage.

When it comes to vision coverage, Medicare does provide typical medical coverage for conditions, injuries, and illnesses of the eye. Part B covers the treatment of glaucoma and cataracts like any other health condition. It is the routine vision services that Medicare doesn't cover. Beneficiaries need to plan to pay for this coverage for themselves. (Some Medicare Advantage plans offer limited benefits for these items, which we discuss in a later chapter. You can also purchase standalone dental, vision, and hearing insurance to help pay for these expenses.)

Non-Medicare Home Care

At some point, you or your family may think you need home health care. Medicare provides only very limited benefits for this, and there are strict qualification rules. For example, *if you are homebound and under your physician's care,* he or she may order intermittent skilled-nursing care for you. A certified Medicare home health agency must deliver this care and do it within 21 days or less. (Medicare can extend the limit in exceptional circumstances.) You would pay for any additional home care outside of this. Also, you can't just hire any home health aide and expect Medicare to pay for it because you think you need help. I've seen people rack up thousands of dollars of expenses for this type of care without realizing that Medicare would not be paying for it. Your doctor must request it, the help or aide must be from a certified Medicare agency, and Medicare must approve the request. While providing skilled care, the health aides provided by the agency *may* also help with *custodial types of care* (see below) that are related to your injury or illness recovery. But again, you may not qualify for skilled care. Even if you do, Medicare covers that care only for a short time.

Long-Term-Care Costs

While Medicare does provide up to 100 days of coverage in a skilled nursing facility (SNF) when medically necessary, this coverage does not extend to long-term-care costs associated with an assisted-living facility or nursing home. SNF care is provided by Medicare Part A to help people recover after an inpatient hospital stay. In other words, Medicare covers this care to help people get on their feet and back to caring for themselves.

Medicare doesn't typically cover *custodial care* such as cooking, cleaning, or help with the "normal activities of daily living" (such as bathing, dressing, toileting, and eating). In limited circumstances, you may have a nurse providing skilled care who happens to do a bit of help around the house for you while he or she is there. However, this is an exception and not the normal rule. You should not expect the nurse to perform these activities.

When you are not able to care for yourself independently any longer, you will need to pay for the monthly rent in an assisted living facility or nursing home. Costs for nursing home care can exceed more than $7,000 a month. You would do well to plan carefully as more than 1 in 2 people will eventually need some form of long-term care. Long-term-care insurance is available for purchase if you enroll in it while you are still healthy enough to qualify, but it's pricey. The premiums are usually indexed to your age and health at the time of purchase. Many people don't think of it until it's too late. Medicaid coverage of long-term care is also a last resort when most of your finances have been exhausted. Speaking of Medicaid, let's quickly differentiate that from Medicare.

Medicare vs. Medicaid

Medicare is the federal health insurance program for people aged 65 and older or people under 65 who have a qualifying disability. It's the program that this book is all about.

Medicaid, on the other hand, has no age requirements. *Medicaid is a joint federal and state program that provides health coverage for people of all ages with limited income and assets. These are generally people who otherwise couldn't afford coverage.*

> Gordon has retired without any investments or savings. Most months, he gets by on just his Social Security retirement benefits. Sometimes, he must make choices between food and medication. He applies for Medicaid in his home state of Texas. The state approves his application and deems him a Qualified Medicare Beneficiary (QMB), which is considered full Medicaid. His Medicaid benefits will now pay for his Medicare Parts B and contribute toward his Part D premiums as well. When seeing doctors that accept both Medicare and Medicaid, he also has little to no out-of-pocket spending on health-care services because Medicaid functions as his secondary coverage.

It is possible to have both Medicare and Medicaid at the same time. There are millions of people who qualify for both. In that scenario, Medicare is primary, and Medicaid is secondary, which means you do not necessarily need to buy a Medigap plan. Medicaid may even help to pay for your Parts B and D premiums and most of your Medicare cost-sharing expenses. You will, however, need to enroll in Part D. In fact, if a Medicare beneficiary who is also a Medicaid recipient fails to enroll in a Part D plan, Medicare will choose a plan and automatically enroll him or her.

Medicaid also offers some benefits not found in Medicare. These include help with the costs of personal care or the long-term-care costs we discussed earlier. We won't go too far into Medicaid as it is outside the scope of this book. However, if you believe you have income low enough to qualify, you should contact your local Department of Health and Human Services.

And that brings us to the end of this chapter on the basics of Medicare. Congratulations! You've now learned what Medicare covers, and more importantly, what it costs. This puts you well ahead of the hundreds of beneficiaries we meet each year who make Medicare Mistakes #1 and #2.

There is considerably more that I could tell you about what Medicare costs and covers. For example, we could get into the "soft caps" on physical therapy, or I could tell you how you need to use approved vendors for things like diabetes supplies. We could also get into Medicare denials and appeals and grievances.

As I mentioned earlier, though, we don't want to put the cart before the horse. I've designed this book to give you the basics you need to know to get started, and we'll leave it at that. All of that other stuff is information I can provide you in other formats once you've mastered the basics and enrolled in suitable coverage.

Wouldn't you agree that learning just these basics is already a challenge?

We have other reading resources for you once you master these basics, so it's time to move on to how you'll determine the best time to enroll.

Key Takeaways

- Medicare covers a portion of your health-care costs. You cover the rest in the form of deductibles, copays, and coinsurance.
- A deductible is the amount of money you will pay out of your pocket before your benefits kick in.
- A copay or coinsurance is your share of a covered health-care expense after you have met the deductible.
- The Medicare Part A deductible is $1,484 per benefit period. You can pay this more than once in a calendar year if you have more than one benefit period.
- If your inpatient hospital stay is longer than 60 days, you will pay daily hospital copays, which grow with time. Benefits run out if you exhaust your lifetime reserve days, which are days 91 – 150. After that, you pay all costs unless you have supplemental coverage to provide additional days.
- The Medicare Part B deductible is $203 per calendar year.
- After the Part B deductible, Medicare pays 80%, while you cover the other 20%, which is your coinsurance.
- You pay that 20% forever unless you have supplemental coverage to pay it for you.

- Medicare does not cover routine vision, dental, or hearing care.
- Medicare does not cover long-term care.
- Medicare and Medicaid are two different programs. Medicaid provides health coverage for people with limited incomes. Some people have both.

BOOMER BENEFITS PRO TIP: Many of our clients have told us that things began to make sense when they learned about Medicare in more than one format—for example, reading about Medicare and also watching our Medicare videos. We've included some these resources for you in our book bonus, so check them out in Chapter 12.

MAJOR DECISION:

When Is Your Best Time to Enroll?

Chapter
3

MEDICARE MISTAKE #3:

Missing Your Initial Enrollment Period (IEP)

Medicare has specific enrollment periods that govern when you can enroll, change, or disenroll from certain coverages. Becoming familiar with them will help you avoid late penalties and unexpected medical bills. As you near age 65, you will encounter the first and most important of these, which is called your *Initial Enrollment Period* (or IEP). The federal government gives you a 7-month window to sign up for Medicare. **The decisions you make during that window will affect you for the rest of your life.**

This used to be so much easier back in the 1960s when Congress created Medicare. Back then, most people retired by age

65, so nearly everyone signed up for Medicare when they first became eligible. In today's world, however, many people work well past age 65, because they want to and can earn delayed retirement credits that will increase the amount of their future Social Security check. That's all fine and good on its own. However, they often assume things about their Medicare enrollment that they shouldn't without realizing the stiff penalties that can result from their assumptions.

Medicare Mistake #3: Missing Your Initial Enrollment Period (IEP)

Everyone gets an Initial Enrollment Period for Medicare that is specific to them. Medicare expects you to know whether you should enroll right at 65 and also which parts you should enroll in regardless of whether you are still working. You can delay certain parts of Medicare without penalty in some employment situations but not in others. If you get it wrong, you may experience coverage gaps, delays, and financial penalties that can stick with you for life.

In this chapter, I'll help you determine the best time for you to enroll based on your employment status. I'll also help you decide which parts of Medicare you personally need to enroll in because not everyone needs all four parts.

Your Initial Enrollment Period for Medicare

Your IEP begins three months before the month of your 65th birthday, includes the month of your birthday, and then extends for three months after your birthday month. (See Figure 3-1.)

MEDICARE INITIAL ENROLLMENT PERIOD

3 MONTHS BEFORE

65TH BIRTHDAY MONTH

3 MONTHS AFTER

BEGINS:
Three months before
the month of your
65th birthday

7-MONTH WINDOW

ENDS:
Three months after
the month of your
65th birthday

Figure 3-1.

For example, if you turn 65 on April 20, your Medicare IEP would begin on January 1 and run through July 31.

If Medicare is your *primary coverage*—meaning your main source of health insurance—then you need to enroll in *both* Medicare Parts A and B during your IEP. Remember, these two parts together are called Original Medicare. They are the only parts that you will sign up for through Social Security (or the Railroad Retirement Board).

Don't expect Medicare to notify you when it's time to sign up. We meet people all the time who are surprised that they never received anything from Medicare to inform them that it was time to sign up. That's because the government expects you to have done your research and know when to enroll. The Social Security office enrolls some people automatically, but not others. To make it simple for you, here's what you need to know:

Taking Social Security benefits already? They will automatically enroll you in Parts A and B.

Not receiving Social Security benefits yet? You must enroll yourself.

we did [handwritten margin note]

FAQ: Why does your Social Security income status make a difference?

ANSWER: If you are already taking Social Security income (or Railroad Retirement) benefits, the government assumes you have retired. They also suspect you may no longer have any employer coverage. Therefore, they will automatically enroll you in Medicare Parts A and B at age 65.

When Social Security auto-enrolls you, your Medicare card will just show up in your mailbox several months before you turn 65. Your Medicare benefits will start on the first of the month in which you turn 65. However, if you aren't getting Social Security benefits yet, Medicare won't mail you any enrollment information. You will need to submit a Medicare application yourself.

To use our online calculator to get the exact dates of your IEP based on *your* birthday, visit our special book bonus page online. You can find information about it in Chapter 12.

IEP EXCEPTIONS AFFECTING PEOPLE BORN ON THE FIRST OF THE MONTH: There is an exception that affects only individuals whose birthday falls on the 1st of any month. For these people, the IEP will start one month early. For example, if your birthday is April 1, your IEP will begin on March 1. Your Medicare benefits can begin as early as March 1, which is one month earlier than beneficiaries who were not born on the first day of the month.

Your Medicare Start Date

Enrolling anytime during your 7-month window will help you avoid a late penalty. However, you may have a specific Medicare effective date that you are aiming for, such as the day after the last day of work at your current employer. If that's the case, you need to know that *the date when* you enroll during the 7-month window will affect your Medicare start date. For example, if you enroll in the first three months of your 7-month window, your Medicare benefits will begin on the first of the month in which you turn 65. Unless, of course, your birthday falls on the first day of the month. Then your benefits begin a month earlier (see exceptions box above this paragraph).

If Medicare is your primary coverage, you should enroll in Medicare in those three months before the month of your birthday so that your benefits will begin the month you turn 65. However, if you enroll in Medicare in the three months after your 65th birthday, then your start date may be delayed. You'll want to know this so you can anticipate any possible gaps in coverage. To see how your application date affects your start date, see Figure 3-2 on the next page.

I should also mention here that when it comes to these later start dates, there seems to be no consistency with the government following this rule. Sometimes the Social Security representative assigns the delayed start date as listed. I've also seen other times where a Social Security representative backdates the effective date for Part B. So, the best way to be certain of your Medicare effective date is to apply before the month in which you turn 65.

Here's something else I want you to be aware of: *Medicare's rules require that your IEP trumps any other election period.* This rule can cause problems for you if you plan to retire in the three months AFTER your 65th birthday while you are still in your IEP.

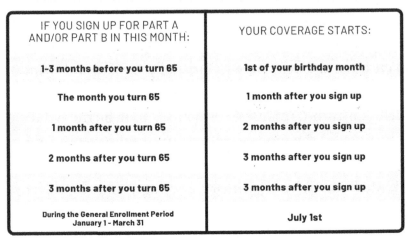

MEDICARE COVERAGE START DATE

IF YOU SIGN UP FOR PART A AND/OR PART B IN THIS MONTH:	YOUR COVERAGE STARTS:
1-3 months before you turn 65	1st of your birthday month
The month you turn 65	1 month after you sign up
1 month after you turn 65	2 months after you sign up
2 months after you turn 65	3 months after you sign up
3 months after you turn 65	3 months after you sign up
During the General Enrollment Period January 1 - March 31	July 1st

Figure 3-2.

Remember earlier when I said that Medicare has various enrollment periods that you can use to enroll in, change, or leave coverage? Well, most of the time, retiring after 65 means you will get a Special Enrollment Period (SEP) to enroll in Medicare to start the day *after* your group coverage ends. However, in this case, the fact that you are still in your 7-month IEP overrides any SEP you may have otherwise had.

Let's say that you wait to enroll in Medicare until two months after your birthday, thinking that your Medicare will start in the month after submitting your application. Unfortunately, you'll find that your Medicare start date is delayed by three months, as indicated in Figure 3-2. This could cause a gap in coverage between your employer coverage ending and your Medicare beginning. Working with an experienced broker who knows the enrollment period rules can help you avoid any mistakes here.

FAQ: So why are election periods significant anyway?

ANSWER: When you use them properly, you'll avoid penalties, which we'll talk about next.

Late Penalties for Original Medicare

It's easy to avoid a late enrollment penalty by enrolling during your IEP. You can also safely delay your enrollment by having other creditable health coverage, usually through a large employer. However, it's astonishing how many people do miss their window and incur a penalty.

Suppose you have no other creditable health coverage, and you **do not** enroll during your 7-month IEP. In that case, you could be subject to a Part B late enrollment penalty. The penalty is cumulative and assessed at 10% for every 12-month period that you fail to enroll in Part B. You'll pay this penalty every month for as long as you remain enrolled in Part B, or in other words, for the rest of your life! It can add up to thousands of dollars.

You may also have a gap in coverage because once you figure out that you missed your window, you can't just enroll any time during the year. You'll have to wait for the next General Enrollment Period (GEP) to sign up. The GEP runs from January 1 to March 31. When you enroll in Part B during the GEP, your coverage doesn't start until the following July.

General Enrollment Period (GEP)
January 1 - March 31

Figure 3-3.

Let's look at an example. Hank was very healthy when he retired at 65, so he never signed up for Medicare. It seemed too expensive at the time. Now he is 67 and needs to see a doctor, so he goes down to the Social Security office in April to sign up. The representative informs him he must wait until the next GEP to apply. The next GEP doesn't start until the following January, and the coverage itself won't begin until July 1 after the enrollment. Now Hank is facing 15 months before he can get Medicare coverage for his doctor visit. As if that weren't bad enough, his late enrollment penalty is 20% because he was late in signing up by more than two full 12-month periods. He will pay the 20% penalty every single month for as long as he remains in Part B, which is likely for the rest of his life. The base Part B premium is $148.50/month, so that would result in a penalty of $29.70/month for someone beginning Medicare late in 2021. However, Part B premiums tend to go up a little each year, so the penalty, being a percentage of the base premium, goes up a little each year as well.

While it won't affect many people, there is also a late enrollment penalty for Part A. This penalty only affects people who are *not* eligible for premium-free Part A. If they don't sign up for Part A when they first become eligible, their premiums can increase by 10%. They must then pay that higher premium for twice the number of years that they could have had Part A but did not. Fortunately, the penalty here doesn't affect many people because most are eligible for premium-free Part A.

You've now learned about your IEP for Medicare. Let's talk now about the most common reason people delay enrollment, which is due to having employer health coverage.

Medicare and Employer Coverage

If you are still working when you turn 65 and have access to employer coverage, you'll have some decisions to make. You can keep your employer insurance and allow Medicare to coordinate with that coverage. You could also leave that coverage and elect Medicare as your primary insurance instead.

Deciding between these two options is a big decision for many people, one that my team walks people through every day. It's tricky because Medicare coordinates differently with your employer coverage based on the size of the employer and whether you are actively working or retired. Doing your research will help you to decide on which coverage option is most cost-effective.

Active Large-Employer Coverage: 20 or More Employees

Let's first look at the most common situation: an employee who works for a large employer with 20 or more employees or a multiemployer group with more than 20 total employees.

Active employer coverage simply means you are still actively working, not retired. When you turn 65 and become eligible for Medicare, you will have the right to remain on your large employer's group health insurance plan if you choose to do so. Your employer cannot force you from their large-employer health coverage. This right exists whether you are getting coverage from your own large employer or a spouse's employer.

When you actively work for a large employer with 20 or more employees, the employer coverage is primary, and Medicare is secondary. Your employer plan pays first, and Medicare pays second if you are 65 or older. (Exceptions: 1. For people on Medicare under 65 due to a disability or health condition, Medicare pays secondary when there are 100 or more employees. 2. Medicare is also secondary for people with End-Stage Renal Disease (ESRD) during a 30-month coordination period).

Because Medicare is secondary when you work for a large employer, you can delay enrollment into Medicare Part B without penalty to save yourself from paying Part B premiums. You can also delay enrollment into Part D without penalty if your employer drug coverage is creditable. *Creditable* means that the drug coverage inside your employer plan is as good as or better than Part D.

Makes sense to delay enrollment, right?

Your employer coverage already provides you with outpatient coverage and drug coverage. Why would you want to pay for Medicare Parts B and D, too? Later, when you retire, Medicare will give you a Special Enrollment Period to pick up Parts B and D.

While you can also delay enrollment into Part A here, most employees working at a large employer that offers health coverage do enroll in Part A during their IEP. Remember, Part A is premium-free for most beneficiaries. It costs nothing to enroll in Part A, and the coverage could help you if you have a hospital stay. For example, let's say your employer's health plan has a $3,000 deductible. The Medicare Part A hospital deductible is $1,484. If you incur several thousand dollars in inpatient charges for a hospital stay, you will pay for only $1,484 of those hospital charges because that is the Part A deductible. Medicare kicks in as your secondary coverage and pays the rest of any Part A service charges over that amount.   — *stopped 1/2021*

I will mention one exception here: *If you are contributing to a health savings account (HSA) and plan to continue doing so, do not enroll in Part A or any other part of Medicare.* The IRS currently does not allow contributions to a health savings account when you have enrolled in any part of Medicare. Also, you need to know that later when you DO enroll in Part A, Social Security will make your effective date retroactive by six months prior to your **application** date. This means you need to stop contributing to the health savings account a full six months before you apply for Medicare when you are well past your IEP.

BOOMER BENEFITS PRO TIP: The key word here is "apply." One member of our Medicare Q&A Facebook group shared that her husband thought the retroactive enrollment date would be six months before the Medicare effective date. However, when processing his enrollment, his local Social Security office made his effective date retroactive to his application date, which was two months prior to his intended effective date. He then had to work with his HSA administrator to take money back out of his HSA because his Medicare effective date started earlier than he had stopped contributing. Tricky stuff, especially when different Social Security offices seem to make different decisions on these things! My advice: stop contributing six months before you sign up. Then you will know that your contributions won't coincide with whatever effective date they put on your actual card.

first 1/6/2021

If you have employer coverage with a health savings account, check out our video about Medicare and HSA Plans here: https://boomerbenefits.link/watch-HSA.

We also created a handy HSA Flow Chart for you if you need it. It will help you with when to stop contributing to your HSA when you ARE ready to transition to Medicare. You can find it here: https://boomerbenefits.link/HSA-Chart.

Last, there are a few special employer situations that fall outside of the general discussion. If you suspect that your situation might be different, check out Medicare's guide on benefits coordination:

https://www.medicare.gov/Pubs/pdf/02179-medicare-coordination-benefits-payer.pdf.

Delaying Parts B and D with Large-Employer Coverage

Sometimes, people with high deductibles on their employer plan want the extra Part B coverage to work alongside it. If that's you, fine. It might benefit you if you meet your employer deductible often for ongoing outpatient medical costs.

However, you'll want to consider the costs of Part B in this scenario. After all, the base premium for Part B is $148.50/month. That is $1,782/year that you can keep in your pocket by delaying Part B until later when you leave that large-employer coverage.

Later, when you are ready to retire, you will qualify for a Special Enrollment Period to enroll in Part B with no penalty. You will need to go down to your local Social Security office with an "**Application for Part B**" and a "**Request for Employment Information**" m that your employer HR department can complete for you.

You can find both forms online at www.cms.gov, so you should
complete them ahead of time. The application for Part B is "CMS
Form 40B." The Employment verification form is "CMS- L564."
Take a copy of your creditable coverage letter from your former
insurer as well if you have already received it.

If your drug coverage inside your employer plan was creditable and you maintained that drug coverage consistently since
you turned 65, you'll also have a two-month Special Enrollment
Period to enroll in Part D with no penalty.

> **FAQ:** How do I know if my employer drug coverage is creditable?
>
> **Answer:** The employer must notify you annually in writing if the drug
> coverage is not creditable so that you can pick up a Part D drug plan
> and avoid a Part D late enrollment penalty.

Inactive Large-Employer Coverage: COBRA

The Consolidated Omnibus Budget Reconciliation Act, also
known as COBRA, enables people to extend their employer
coverage for 18 to 36 months beyond the date when they lose
that coverage.

*Medicare coordinates differently with COBRA than it does with
active employer coverage.* It depends on which coverage you had
first. **If you are already enrolled** in COBRA prior to becoming
eligible for Medicare, then you usually cannot stay on COBRA
(and you probably won't want to anyway because Medicare is
usually considerably less expensive). Your COBRA will end on
the date that your Medicare begins, so you'll want to enroll in
both Medicare Parts A and B during your IEP. However, your

dependents can keep COBRA for up to 36 months even though you are transitioning to Medicare.

If you are enrolled in Medicare Parts A or B before you become eligible for COBRA, you have the option to enroll in COBRA if you want to. Perhaps you have some expensive medications. You feel that COBRA is a better option for you than a Medigap plan and Part D. That's fine but be aware that COBRA is secondary to Medicare. Medicare pays first, so you need both Parts A and B. If you just had Part A before, you must enroll in Part B no later than your 8th month on COBRA insurance. Losing your active-employer coverage will trigger your Part B Special Enrollment Period, which only lasts eight months. *Failure to enroll in Part B within that 8-month window* *can result in a permanent late enrollment penalty for Part B.* It

---

COORDINATING COBRA AND MEDICARE: THE WRONG WAY

Donald decided to continue working at his large employer. When he turned 65, he enrolled in Part A as secondary coverage to his large-employer health plan. Five years later, he retires and enrolls in COBRA because he has some expensive medications. He wants to keep his employer coverage for as long as possible. He assumes he doesn't need to enroll in Medicare Part B until COBRA is exhausted. Eighteen months later, he attempts to sign up for Part B and learns that he has to wait until the next General Enrollment Period. This leaves him without coverage for months. He also gets smacked with a late penalty for life because he failed to sign up for Part B within eight months of his last workday.

COORDINATING COBRA AND MEDICARE: THE RIGHT WAY

Donald decided to continue working at his large employer. When he turned 65, he enrolled in Part A as secondary coverage to his large-employer health plan. Five years later, when he retires and enrolls in COBRA, he also signs up for Medicare Part B to avoid a late penalty since Medicare is primary to COBRA.

could also delay your Medicare Part B until July of the following year if you have to wait for the next General Enrollment Period. You do not want to find yourself in a situation where you must wait months before your Part B begins.

The Option to Choose Medicare as Your Primary Insurance

FAQ: Can I leave my employer coverage to choose Medicare as my primary insurance instead?

ANSWER: You can leave your employer coverage and choose Medicare as your primary insurance instead. (Be sure you check with your employer to confirm if you must wait to leave their group health plan during the plan's next open enrollment period). Then you would just add a Medigap plan or Medicare Advantage plan to round out your coverage.

However, I would caution you to run the numbers carefully. Because your employer contributes toward the cost of your company health insurance premiums, Medicare may cost you more than staying on your group plan. On the other hand, if you are carrying your spouse on your employer plan, we sometimes find that moving *your spouse* to Medicare IS a good option. Many employers don't contribute toward the cost of carrying dependents on the employer plan. That means your Medicare-age spouse could cost you a lot in payroll deductions.

Here's a general rule of thumb: If your employer group coverage costs you very little and has plentiful benefits, you'll likely want to stick with that coverage. You can delay your enrollment into Medicare. On the other hand, perhaps your employer coverage costs you a lot in payroll deductions or has a high deductible. These things could cause quite a bit of medical spending for you each year. You may find that Medicare and a Medigap or Advantage plan is more cost-effective for you. The plan's deductible and copays and your medication usage are all factors you should consider, especially if you take brand-name medications. The free help of a Medicare broker can benefit you, as we know what to look for and what factors to compare.

Another consideration is dependents. If your spouse is younger than you, you may want to stay on your employer's plan to continue coverage for your spouse until he or she becomes eligible for Medicare. Your spouse would lose coverage when you leave your employer plan and obtain private coverage through the Healthcare Exchange instead. Individual coverage is not cheap unless your income is low enough to qualify for an Affordable Care Act subsidy.

> Heather has large-employer coverage with a $2,000 deductible. Because her employer contributes 80% of the employee premiums, Heather's payroll deductions for her coverage are only about $100/month. However, her employer does not contribute to the cost of her spouse's coverage. Her payroll deductions for Hank's coverage are nearly $500/month. Heather should run the numbers to see if Medicare and a Medigap plan or Medicare Advantage plan might be more cost-effective for covering Hank. See Figure 3-4 below.

Last, if you *do* intend to make a move to Medicare, check with your employer first. Find out if you must wait for the employer group plan's open enrollment period to disenroll from that coverage. Some group plans allow you to exit only during the plan's annual open enrollment window.

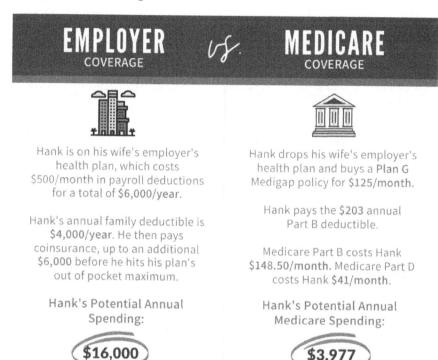

Figure 3-4.

Small-Employer Coverage: Under 20 Employees

How your small-employer coverage coordinates with Medi-care **is the opposite** *of how Medicare coordinates with active large-employer coverage.* **If your employer has fewer than 20 employees, Medicare is primary, and your employer plan is secondary.** In this situation, you should enroll in both Parts A and B when you turn 65 because Medicare will pay first. Failing to enroll in PRIMARY coverage means that you could be on the hook for medical bills that Medicare would have covered if you had enrolled at 65 like you were supposed to.

This is exactly what happened to Janet. Janet had spent the last ten years of her career as a bookkeeper for a small company and enjoyed her job. For this reason, she decided to work past age 65 for a few years. Very healthy and taking no medications, Janet rarely used her company's employer coverage. She liked the coverage well enough, though, so she didn't enroll in Medicare when she turned 65.

The next year, her orthopedic physician scheduled her for knee surgery. When she called her employer insurance coverage for prior authorization, she received some terrible news: Her insurance company would cover only 20% of the surgery cost. This is because Medicare is primary when you work for a small employer with less than 20 employees. The representative informed her that Medicare Part B was responsible for the other 80%. Of course, she had never enrolled in Part B.

How did she go so wrong?

Janet had gotten her advice about her Medicare enrollment from a friend who had worked past age 65 himself at a large company. The friend's employer benefits representative had told him that he didn't need to sign up for Medicare because he had employer coverage. That was fine for him since large-employer coverage is primary to Medicare. The mistake is that neither he nor Janet ever considered that small-employer coverage might not coordinate with Medicare the same way.

It didn't. And there's more.

Occasionally, we see insurance companies who say they will cover Medicare's share of the claims even if you don't enroll in

Part B. **Don't take their word for it.** You run the risk of that insurance company changing that benefit at any time without warning and leaving you stuck with all the expenses that Part B would typically cover. It's not worth the risk.

At Boomer Benefits, we get calls regularly from panicked individuals who were unaware that Medicare pays primary when you work for a small employer. They never enrolled, and they only find out when they now owe 80% of the cost of their outpatient surgery or expensive CT scan. Now they are desperately searching for answers online as to how they could have made this monumental mistake.

Moral of the story for employees at small companies: We recommend that you enroll in Parts A and B at 65 to avoid all of these potential mishaps.

Should You Keep Your Small Group Insurance?

Employees at smaller companies often pay a substantially higher portion of the cost of their employer group plan. Smaller employers may have less money to allocate toward benefits like group health insurance. It's not unusual for us to run into these employees who are contributing more than $300/month toward their employer coverage, which will now pay secondary.

There are still deductibles to meet and copays to pay on that employer plan. In this scenario, you might save money by leaving the employer coverage and enrolling in a Medigap plan or a Medicare Advantage plan instead of sticking with your employer plan. Again, you'll want to run the numbers.

Over the years, we have assisted many people who were paying hundreds of dollars for a group plan with a huge deductible and $40+ doctor copays. Moving to Medicare and a Medigap plan was advantageous for these folks. They saved significantly on premiums and lowered their deductible exposure.

Recap: Medicare and Employer Coverage

Now, I just went over a whole bunch of information about how Medicare coordinates with employer coverage, so let's do a quick recap.

MEDICARE & EMPLOYER COVERAGE

LARGE EMPLOYER = 20+ EMPLOYEES   SMALL EMPLOYER = <20 EMPLOYEES

Medicare is <u>secondary</u> if you are age 65 or older and your employer has <u>more than 20</u> employees and you are ACTIVELY working.

Medicare is <u>primary</u> if you are age 65 or older and your employer has <u>fewer than 20</u> employees.

Figure 3-5.

If you actively work for a large employer with 20 or more employees, you can enroll in just Part A. Part A will pay secondary to your employer coverage and could lower your out-of-pocket costs if you have an inpatient stay. You can delay Parts B and D to save on those premiums unless your employer notifies you that their drug coverage is NOT as good as Medicare, which is rare. Later, when you leave that coverage, you'll have a Special Enrollment Period to enroll in those parts without penalty.

If you actively work for a small employer with less than 20 employees or you have COBRA, you should enroll in both Medicare Parts A and B, since Medicare will pay primary. Doing so will ensure that you don't unknowingly end up on the hook for paying 80% of outpatient services.

In either case, you can leave your employer coverage to choose Medicare as primary instead. However, you should only do so if that makes sense financially.

Now let's move on to discuss retiree coverage.

Retiree Coverage

Medicare beneficiaries who have access to retiree coverage, TRICARE for Life (TFL), or Federal Employee Health Benefits (FEHB), generally do not need the help of a Medicare insurance broker like us. They usually do not need to purchase supplemental coverage. However, they often don't know this and will buy books like this one only to find that it doesn't discuss their situation. In case you are in that boat, I wanted to include a few paragraphs with guidance for you here and direct you to some additional resources.

First, if your company offers you retiree coverage *after* you have stopped actively working, count yourself lucky. Fewer and fewer employers provide retiree coverage today. It is quickly becoming a thing of the past. When you have retiree coverage from a former employer, **Medicare is primary** to that coverage.

You need to enroll in Medicare Parts A and B when you first become eligible.

Speak with the administrator of your retiree coverage to find out the costs for maintaining that coverage. If rates are high, you can consider leaving the retiree coverage for a Medigap and Part D drug plan. However, leaving that coverage may prevent you from returning to it in the future. It's not a decision to make lightly.

Samuel worked for his employer for nearly 40 years and is eligible for inexpensive retiree health-care benefits when he retires at age 65. He signs up for both Medicare Parts A and B during his IEP for Medicare because he knows Medicare will be his primary coverage. He does not need a private market Medigap plan because his retiree coverage will pay secondary to Medicare.

Some employers offer retiree coverage in the form of a group Medicare Advantage plan. You will get your retiree benefits by enrolling in the Medicare Advantage plan offered to retirees by your former employer. For some people, this option works well. Still, if your doctors don't participate in the Advantage plan's network, you may want to leave the retiree plan and enroll in a Medigap and Part D plan so that you can keep your preferred doctors. It's up to you.

TRICARE for Life

TRICARE is the health program for uniformed service members. TRICARE for Life is their program that coordinates with Medicare, wrapping around Medicare's coverage. When you retire from the military, you become eligible for

TRICARE for Life (TFL). Medicare is primary in this scenario, so you'll need to sign up for Medicare Parts A and B at 65. Your TFL benefits will pay secondary to Medicare. Your TFL coverage will start on the first day that both Parts A and B become active.

TFL functions as a supplement, or wraparound, for people who have enrolled in Medicare Parts A and B. Your providers will send their bills to Medicare. After Medicare pays its portion of your bills, it will forward the rest of that claim to TRICARE for processing. The result is that TFL acts very much like a Medigap plan. But since you do not pay premiums for TFL, it will cost you less than a Medigap plan.

TRICARE also recommends that you keep your personal information up to date in the Defense Enrollment Eligibility Reporting System (DEERS) so that they can deliver your benefits promptly.

TFL also includes prescription drug coverage, which you can use instead of Medicare Part D. You can learn more about TFL here: https://tricare.mil/tfl

Some people with TFL decide to enroll in a Medicare Advantage plan for some of the extras that they might gain from certain plans, such as dental, vision, and hearing coverage. TFL will even sometimes pay for some of the expenses not paid by your Medicare Advantage plan, such as copays, coinsurance, and deductibles. This is a personal choice, and you should carefully review your options. If you decide to go this route, you should choose a Medicare Advantage plan that does not include Part D, since TFL already includes drug coverage.

Veterans Affairs (VA) Benefits

Technically, VA benefits are not retiree coverage, so we get many questions from veterans on what they should do about Medicare.

FAQ: Should I enroll in Medicare if I have VA benefits?

ANSWER: In my opinion, yes, but it's up to you.

While veterans can choose to get their treatment solely from the VA, their level of benefits varies. The person's length of military service, income level, disabilities related to service, and the VA's resources can all affect what benefits they receive.

The VA assigns a priority level to those who qualify for coverage, with 1 being the highest priority. Your priority level is what determines the type of medical benefits you will have access to. People assigned a level 8 priority could find they have the least coverage, so they have the most to gain by enrolling in Medicare benefits.

The VA website itself states that VA and Medicare are separate and generally do not coordinate coverage. If a person has a nonemergency situation, he or she can request that the VA authorize services in a non-VA hospital. Still, even if it is approved, VA insurance does not pay for all services.

Medicare's website also has a similar disclaimer on its page about VA coverage. *"To get the U.S. Department of Veterans Affairs (VA) to pay for services, you must go to a VA facility or have the VA authorize services in a non-VA facility."* The VA website clarifies that VA benefits are not considered health insurance and encourages veterans to enroll in Medicare.

Suppose you are a veteran and want to seek treatment from non-VA doctors and hospitals. In that case, you should consider signing up for Medicare Parts A and B. The two coverages don't exactly coordinate in the way that Medicare and employer coverage do, but having both will give you some choices in where you receive your care.

> **FAQ:** What happens if I have VA coverage and don't sign up for Medicare Part B when I'm first eligible but later wish to enroll?
>
> **ANSWER:** You could face late enrollment penalties and a delayed start date for Part B.

Veterans should also consider enrolling in Part D because the VA doesn't cover all medications. You usually can't fill a prescription through the VA pharmacy unless a VA doctor prescribed it.

My dad is a Vietnam-era veteran and qualifies for VA health benefits. Still, after I reviewed all his coverage options, I advised him to enroll him in Medicare Parts A and B, a Part D drug plan, and a high-deductible Medigap plan. I wanted him to have adequate health-care options, and I have not regretted that decision. Sure enough, he soon learned that the VA doesn't cover two of his expensive brand-name prescriptions. It isn't a problem, though, because he can get them filled through the standalone Part D drug plan that I helped him select. Had he not enrolled in that Part D plan, those two medications together would have cost him over $700/month out of pocket. I never want him to have to choose between the right medication and the medication that he can afford.

The Medicare coverage I set up for him gives him, and me, the peace of mind that he has adequate drug coverage. It also assures me that if he decides to pursue civilian treatment, his Medigap plan will limit his spending. I also know that he won't spend hours or days or weeks waiting for an appointment at the VA when he needs medical treatment. While many VA clinics provide prompt treatment, the waiting times at other clinics have made national news in years past. Take all these things into consideration if you are a veteran.

Last, some veterans choose to enroll in a Medicare Advantage plan that offers extras like gym memberships. A greater benefit of these plans is that they can use the VA whenever they want to, but when they want to see a civilian doctor, they can use the network of providers available to them through their Medicare Advantage plan. We'll discuss Medicare Advantage plans further in Chapter 7.

Federal Employee Health Benefits (FEHB)

Our agency gets hundreds of questions about FEHB every year. In fact, we get so many questions that we have even created a basic video about FEHB and Medicare on our YouTube channel. It gives federal retirees a starting point, even though we don't sell or service these plans.

FEHB retirees who are entitled to Part A without paying premiums should enroll as it can't hurt and might help. However, it is up to you whether you choose to enroll in Part B since you'll have monthly premiums associated with Part B based on your income. Just be aware that if you don't enroll in Part B when you are first eligible, you'll pay the applicable late-enrollment penalty if you later decide to enroll in it.

The Office of Personnel Management has put together a great page that explains everything you need to know about the coordination of Medicare and FEHB benefits. You can find a list of frequently asked questions and a link to the FEHB and Medicare booklet here: https://www.opm.gov/healthcare-insurance/healthcare/medicare/coordination-of-medicare-and-fehb-benefits/

That's a pretty long URL to type into your browser, so don't hesitate to find it by just typing the phrase "FEHB and Medicare" into your internet browser.

In California, they have a public employee retirement system. If you live in California and are entitled to CalPERS, visit their website for information eligibility and enrollment related to Medicare: https://www.calpers.ca.gov/page/retirees/health-and-medicare/medicare

Additional Resources for Retiree, FEHB, VA, and TRICARE

If you have employer-sponsored retiree coverage, FEHB, VA, or TRICARE benefits, you can also check out the on-demand webinar that we put together specifically to help you. Find it here: https://boomerbenefits.com/medicare-for-fehb-va-tricare-webinar/

Do you have an employer coverage situation that we didn't cover in this chapter? Join us in our free private Facebook group. We answer questions free of charge for Medicare beneficiaries

like you every day. You can find it here: https://www.facebook.
com/groups/BoomerBenefits/

Individual Coverage through the Affordable Care Act (ACA)

There's one last type of pre-65 coverage that we see more
frequently these days, and that's a personal health insurance
policy purchased through the HealthCare Exchange.

The ACA legislation made individual health insurance plans
more affordable for people whose income is below a certain
limit. These people can qualify for a government subsidy that
reduces the cost of that insurance. It's not uncommon for us to
meet people who at age 64 are paying less than $100/month for
their ACA health plan because the tax credits they qualify for
pay most of the premiums for them.

If you've benefited from such a health insurance subsidy, you
may feel hesitant about leaving your inexpensive individual
health insurance plan. However, our legislators never intended
for you to keep an ACA plan over Medicare. If you qualify for
premium-free Medicare Part A, as most do, you should sign up
for Medicare when you first become eligible. Here's why:

You'll Pay Back the Tax Credits You Receive for an ACA Health Plan

Once you become eligible for premium-free Part A, you will
no longer be eligible for a premium tax credit (*subsidy*). If you
keep your ACA plan, you must begin paying the full price for
that plan with no government help. Paying the full monthly
premium for your ACA plan will likely cost far more than what
you would pay for Medicare.

The federal government may not at first catch the fact that

you've continued collecting a subsidy you are no longer eligible for, but eventually, they will. Then you'll get a giant bill requiring you to pay back subsidies that you took advantage of when you were no longer eligible for them.

You Could Face Medicare Delays and Penalties

Even worse, if you fail to enroll in Medicare during your IEP, you could face a delay in your Medicare coverage. Remember that if you miss your IEP, you may have to wait until the next GEP to sign up. (As a reminder, the GEP runs from January 1 to March 31 each year.) However, the coverage won't begin until the following July. This can result in late enrollment penalties that will stay with you for as long as you remain enrolled in Medicare.

FAQ: When should I cancel my ACA coverage if I am enrolling in Medicare?

ANSWER: You should call the Healthcare Exchange and notify them to cancel your ACA plan sometime in the last month before your Medicare coverage begins. You do not need both coverages. It's illegal for an insurance carrier or agent to sell you a Marketplace plan if you have either Medicare Part A or Part B. Cancellation is not automatic, though, so you need to cancel your ACA coverage yourself.

Failing to transition over to Medicare at age 65 is a costly error that has been made by thousands of people. To prevent future beneficiaries from making the same mistake, the Center for Medicare and Medicaid Services now sends letters to ACA enrollees before they turn 65.

Exceptions Regarding ACA and Medicare Coverage

As usual, there are a couple of exceptions to what I've explained in the previous sections. The small percentage of people who pay Part A premiums can choose to keep their ACA coverage. They would still owe a late penalty for Part B if they later decided to enroll in a few years down the road.

People with End-Stage Renal Disease are also not required to enroll in Medicare. If you have ESRD and have not yet enrolled in Part A or B, you can choose a Marketplace plan instead. People with ESRD might also qualify for subsidies that reduce the monthly premiums for the plan and reduced cost-sharing expenses through the Marketplace. This eligibility for tax credits and cost-sharing reductions will terminate if you later sign up for Part A.

What if You Can't Afford Medicare?

If you live on a fixed income or even just Social Security alone, shelling out $148.50/month (or more) for Medicare Part B can be a financial hardship. If you have money saved up in an HSA, you can use that money to pay for your Medicare Part D and premiums. Another option you can consider is to deduct the cost of Medicare from your taxes if you itemize your taxes and have medical expenses in excess of 7.5 percent of your Adjusted Gross Income. Consult a tax advisor for help.

Medicare also offers several savings programs for people with low incomes. People who qualify for one of the four Savings Programs can get help paying their Medicare premiums and their Medicare deductibles, copays, and coinsurance.

You can find the monthly income and resource limits to

qualify for Medicare Savings Programs here: https://www. medicare.gov/your-medicare-costs/get-help-paying-costs/ medicare-savings-programs

If your income or resources are too high to qualify for one of these, you might still qualify for help with the cost of your prescriptions through the Extra Help for Part D program. This program is also called the Low-Income Subsidy (LIS). When you qualify for Extra Help, you will get assistance with the cost of your Part D costs on several levels that include:

- Reduced Part D premiums
- No deductible
- No coverage gap ("donut hole")
- Reduced copays/coinsurance for your medications

To see if you qualify or to apply for Extra Help, you can get started here: https://www.ssa.gov/benefits/medicare/ prescriptionhelp/

Key Takeaways

It's always heartbreaking when we have to inform Medicare beneficiaries that they missed their Initial Enrollment Period and now have to wait to enroll. However, it's even more upsetting to find yourself in a situation like Janet's, where she failed to sign up for Medicare during her IEP because she didn't know Medicare is primary if you work for a small employer. We see this often – people who thought they took the right steps only to learn later that they didn't.

Having read this chapter and after considering your situation, you should now be able to determine when the best time is for you to enroll. Remember that:

- Your IEP begins three months before the month of your 65th birthday, includes the month of your birthday, and then extends for three months after your birthday month.
- If Medicare is your *primary coverage*—meaning your main source of health insurance—then you need to enroll in *both* Medicare Parts A and B during your IEP.
- People still working can opt for Medicare to coordinate with their group coverage. How it coordinates depends on the size of the employer.
- If you are contributing to an HSA and plan to continue doing so, do not enroll in Part A or any other part of Medicare.
- Medicare coordinates differently with COBRA than it does with active employer coverage.

In summary, here are your choices for which steps to take during your IEP. You can:

- Enroll in both Parts A and B at age 65 because that coverage will be your primary insurance. This includes people with small employer coverage, retiree coverage, or TRICARE-for-Life as well as people who plan to purchase their own supplemental coverage.
- Sign up for just Part A because you have active-employer coverage that is primary to Medicare because the employer has 20 or more employees. Some people with FEHB also choose this option. (Part B is optional in this

scenario but you'll incur a late penalty if you don't enroll during your IEP and later decide to sign up).
- Delay all Parts of Medicare because you are actively contributing to an HSA and want to continue to do so.

You should know that once you enroll in Medicare Parts A and B, you don't need to renew these annually. You will stay enrolled unless you purposely disenroll or fail to pay your Part B premiums.

Last, you may find it helpful to download the CMS Fact Sheet on "Deciding Whether to Enroll in Medicare Part A and Part B When You Turn 65." You can find it at this URL: https://www. cms.gov/Outreach-and-Education/Find-Your-Provider-Type/ Employers-and-Unions/FS3-Enroll-in-Part-A-and-B.pdf

The next decisions I want to walk you through are about your drug coverage. Your window to enroll in Part D is the same window as your IEP for Medicare itself. Missing that window can lead to a late-enrollment penalty if you don't have other creditable coverage.

Part
3

MAJOR DECISION:

Will You Need Prescription Drug Coverage?

2 mo enrollment period - after leaving Employer plan

MEDICARE MISTAKE #4:

Skipping Part D without Having other Coverage

Medicare Part D is the newest part of Medicare. Get this: For nearly half a century, beneficiaries did not have coverage for outpatient prescription medicines. We are thrilled to have it today, even if it's a bit clunky and confusing. Imagine being diabetic and having to pay 100% of the cost of expensive insulins or having emphysema and spending hundreds out-of-pocket each month for your breathing medications. Many people found themselves in these exact situations before Part D came along. It's no coincidence that more than 70% of beneficiaries[1] now participate in the Part D program.

Although it is far better than nothing, Part D isn't perfect. As governments sometimes do, they created a rather unwieldy program with four different phases, a bunch of medication tiers, and in my opinion, too many choices. And when it comes to costs, you will pay your share here, too, in out-of-pocket expenses for medications. Part D also involves annual choices you must make that you don't have to make with Parts A and B. You'll need to do your homework and research your options every fall. ***Nonetheless, skipping Part D is a considerable risk and not one that I recommend.***

Medicare Mistake #4: Skipping Part D without Having other Coverage

You don't have to enroll in Part D if you don't want to. Technically, it is optional coverage.

Sometimes there are legitimate reasons not to enroll in Part D. Maybe you are still working and have drug coverage through your employer plan. Then you will likely delay Part D. Or perhaps you have VA drug coverage and don't mind getting your medicines filled there.

However, if you don't have other drug coverage, Medicare "encourages" you to enroll in Part D by assessing a late penalty if you don't. This penalty grows with time and is highly annoying but failing to join a Part D plan can result in situations far worse than just paying the penalty. There are many medications out there today that can cost tens of thousands of dollars per year without drug coverage.

Even *with* Medicare Part D drug coverage, a Kaiser Family Foundation study in 2019 showed that enrollees can still pay thousands of dollars annually for specialty drugs that treat conditions like cancer, rheumatoid arthritis (RA), multiple sclerosis, and hepatitis C. Their study showed that Part D enrollees could face out-of-pocket costs for certain cancer medications exceeding $8,000 per year[2]. They also cited examples of median annual out-of-pocket costs of $5,471 for the RA drug, Humira, and $6,672 for MS drug, Copaxone.

Just imagine then what those costs would be without Part D! I have personally seen unprepared Medicare beneficiaries face these drug costs on several occasions.

No one can predict when a disease will strike. Spending just a few dollars per month now on even the lowest-premium drug plan offered in your state will ensure that you have access to a plan that includes important classes of medications, like anti-cancer drugs. Without Part D, some of these would be entirely out of reach for most people on Medicare. Let me give you an overview of Part D so that you can see the details on why I *never* recommend skipping it.

Part D is Optional. Sort of.

Although Part D is "technically" optional, there is a late penalty for skipping it when you don't have any other creditable drug coverage. If you fail to enroll when you are first eligible for Part D, you will begin accumulating a penalty that grows with time. You'll then incur this penalty when you do enroll later, which you almost surely will at some point.

Creditable coverage for Part D *is prescription drug coverage that meets a minimum standard set by Medicare.* Your creditable coverage needs to be as good or better than what Part D would provide. Most employer group health plans include drug cover-age that is creditable for Part D. If your coverage isn't as good, they must notify you of this annually so you can choose to pick up better coverage with Part D.

Drug coverage for veterans provided through the VA also qualifies as creditable coverage. If you have VA drug coverage and decide to enroll in Part D later on, you will not incur the late penalty.

A Penalty that Grows with Time

If you have no other creditable drug coverage, you should sign up for Part D during your Initial Enrollment Period (IEP). If you don't, it can be costly. For each month that you don't enroll, your penalty grows by 1% of the national base drug plan premium.

Part D late penalties are cumulative. If you wait five years to enroll, you will owe a 60% penalty on top of your drug plan premium. *You will pay this penalty for as long as you remain enrolled in Part D*. Since the national base premium can increase every year, your penalty over time will also increase. In 2021, the Part D national base premium is $33.06, so a 60% penalty would tack on nearly $20/month in late fees.

Ouch.

You can avoid the late penalty for Part D by enrolling in drug coverage during your IEP—the same 7-month window during which you sign up for Original Medicare.

If you are working past 65 and have enrolled in Part A or Part B but delayed Part D because you have creditable drug coverage through your employer, you will get a 2-month Special Enroll-ment Period after you lose that coverage to enroll in Part D.

There are two ways to enroll in Part D.

1. You can buy a standalone Part D drug plan alongside your Original Medicare benefits and your Medigap plan.
2. You can enroll in a Medicare Advantage plan that includes a built-in Part D drug plan. (We'll cover Medicare Advantage plans in a later chapter.)

Why Do You Need Part D?

Enrolling in Part D will serve two purposes: 1. you avoid the penalty, and 2. you have coverage midyear if you develop an illness that requires outpatient medications. Many people fail to realize this second reason. You can only enroll in Part D during your IEP or during a valid election period, which for most people comes around only once per year. If you don't enroll during your IEP, your next opportunity won't likely happen until the Annual Election Period (AEP) in the fall, which runs from October 15 to December 7. Having no coverage can spell disaster if you develop a midyear illness requiring expensive medications.

Annual Election Period (AEP)
October 15 - December 7

Figure 4-1.

On 2 mo. after leaving Employer plan

FAQ: I'm healthy and don't take any medications. Should I still enroll in Part D?

ANSWER: In my opinion, yes. You may not want to spend money on drug coverage if you take no medications currently. However, none of us know when we might get sick and need expensive brand-name medications.

Let me give you an example to demonstrate why you need Part D coverage. A few years ago, one of our existing clients contacted us with sad news. She had purchased a Medigap plan through Boomer Benefits when she first turned 65. She had also listened to our annual recommendations about why Part D is so important.

However, she had been a healthy person all her life. She couldn't bring herself to buy a Part D drug plan when she was not taking any prescription drugs at that time. Year after year, she declined to enroll in Part D during the AEP. Then one year in late summer, she was diagnosed with cancer. Her physician prescribed an oral cancer medication called Gleevec. This medication was an urgent and potentially lifesaving drug for her. However, she was not currently in a valid Part D election period, so she had no choice but to pay for the medication out-of-pocket.

The cost of a 30-day supply of this brand-name medication was $5,600/month. (This drug did not have a generic option at that time, but today, even the generic option is very expensive.) She called our office and said to me, "Well, I finally understand what you have been trying to warn me about all these years regarding my Part D coverage. I'm going to have to pay this out-of-pocket now, aren't I?"

Unfortunately, yes. She incurred catastrophic spending because she *didn't want to spend just a few dollars per month* on an inexpensive Part D plan when she was first eligible. As this true story makes clear, skipping Part D is usually not worth the risk. If you don't take any medications, sign up for one of the least expensive plans in your state to prevent a similar financial catastrophe for yourself.

The good news was that our client had saved diligently for her retirement. She was able to pay more than $20,000 for the drug from September through December. In October, we used her AEP to help her join a Part D drug plan that started on January 1. Still, we can all agree that spending $20,000 for just a 4-month supply of this drug is no fun. She could have easily avoided dipping into her retirement funds by enrolling in a low-premium Part D plan when she turned 65. Not everyone has $20,000 saved up for situations like this. Do you?

Catastrophic Drug Coverage You Can Count On

As this poignant story illustrates so well, you don't buy Part D just for the medications you are currently taking. You are buying insurance coverage for future drug needs.

Part D has a *catastrophic coverage limit* that greatly reduces your medication costs once you pass a certain level of covered drug spending in a calendar year. This limit is hands-down the best part of the coverage. It helps to protect Medicare beneficiaries like you from potentially facing medical bankruptcy due to expensive medications.

Part D coverage worked beautifully for my client once it was in place. She filled her Gleevec in January on her new drug plan. Just a one-month supply of her medication caused her to hit the catastrophic limit almost immediately. For the rest of the year, she paid only 5% of the drug costs to continue her treatment. This monthly coinsurance was still over $300/month, but $300/month is a heck of a lot more manageable than $5,600/month.

I consider her lucky that this misfortune happened to her in September. Imagine if her doctors had diagnosed her in February. She would have had to pay $5,600/month for that medication for 11 months. Few people have the savings to do that.

I recommend that you protect yourself from scenarios like this. You don't want to risk paying a fortune for a critical medication.

Again, consider enrolling in an inexpensive plan. All of them come with catastrophic coverage. That way, you aren't spending too much, but you have the coverage for a rainy day.

Part D Is not a Moneymaker for Your Agent

Some of you might be reading and thinking, "Of course you recommend Part D because agents get paid to sell Part D."

Let me shed some light on this.

Medicare sets an annual maximum commission that an agent can earn to enroll someone in Part D. These commissions are so low that many agents won't help you enroll in it. They will just send you to 1-800-MEDICARE to let a government representative help you enroll by phone.

In 2021, the average independent agent gets paid $81 (once)

during your first year ever on any Part D policy. After your first year, the agent's commission is reduced 50% for any renewals of your drug plan (or any other drug plan) that your agent helps you to change to in the future.

In summary, the agent gets paid $41 per YEAR after your first year of coverage (or a little over $3/month). An agent would have to write thousands of Part D drug plans just to make a living. I assure you; no agent is getting rich from enrolling people into Part D.

Furthermore, Part D is very time-intensive for your agent. The back-end involvement is high because there are many common problems with Part D coverage. You will regularly reach out to your agent for help in solving these. For example, pharmacies charge the wrong copay, or the insurance company requires an exception from your doctor. Sometimes your plan refuses to provide the quantity of medication that you need. The list of hassles goes on.

Helping clients resolve these problems often takes hours of an agent's time in conference calls between your insurance company, your doctor, and your pharmacy. While larger agencies like ours have the necessary staff and infrastructure to help our policyholders with such calls, many smaller agencies may not. Earning just $3 each month for a policy that will require time and effort to service doesn't motivate an agent to sell Part D products. Please believe me when I tell you that we don't recommend Part D to fatten our wallets. We recommend it because, without it, you might incur catastrophic drug costs. We see it too often, and it's heartbreaking.

I hope I've convinced you to consider enrolling in Part D for your own sake.

Now, let's look at how Part D works. If you find it overwhelming, don't worry. Even agents find it baffling when they first begin learning about Part D. What I want you to remember as you go through this information is:

- You don't have to become a Part D expert to find the right plan.
- There are tools provided by Medicare to help you choose a suitable plan.
- All policies have federal minimum standards to ensure you get adequate coverage.

You can only have one Part D plan at a time, and all of them follow a standard minimum level of coverage set by Medicare itself. Many drug plans will offer more than the standard minimum during certain phases of the plan. The most important thing is to choose a plan that covers your medications on its list of covered medications, called a *drug formulary*. I'll give you an excellent resource for choosing the right Part D plan after explaining some of the basics about how Part D works.

The Four Phases of Part D

Your Part D drug plan will have four phases that occur when you have reached a certain level of spending:

1. a deductible
2. an initial coverage phase

3. a coverage gap (sometimes called "the donut hole" by beneficiaries)
4. a catastrophic coverage phase

Most recipients never progress beyond the initial coverage phase. They either don't take any medications or take inexpensive generic drugs. Therefore, their spending never crosses the threshold for the coverage gap.

What Is the Tier Structure for Part D Drug Plans?

Part D plans typically categorize their medications into several tiers. Each tier has a copay or coinsurance associated with it that you will pay based on which of the four phases you are in when you fill the medication.

The tiers will range from low-cost preferred generics to costly specialty drugs. Most generic drugs fall in the lower tiers. However, not all generic drugs are cheap. The Part D insurance company can choose to put a generic drug in a higher tier if it's an expensive medication. We often see drugs in the lowest tier cost anywhere from a $0 copay to a $5 copay per prescription. Then the copays go up from there on the other tiers, and your copays will vary by plan.

Your plan will provide you a "Summary of Benefits" that lists the copays/coinsurance that you can expect to pay whenever you fill a medication in that tier. Here's an example of what you might see in a plan's "Summary of Benefits." These are the prices you will pay at the pharmacy during the initial coverage phase (after you have met the deductible):

TIERS	INITIAL COVERAGE	COVERAGE GAP	CATASTROPHIC COVERAGE
Preferred Generic	$1.00 copay	**Generic drugs:** 25%	**Generic drugs:** $3.70 copay or 5% (whichever costs more)
Generic	$7.00 copay		
Preferred Brand	$42.00 copay	**Brand-name drugs:** 25%	**Brand-name drugs:** $9.20 copay or 5% (whichever costs more)
Non-Preferred Drug	35%		
Specialty Tier	25%		

Figure 4-2. Example of Part D Tiers.

Many plans also have two sets of tiered pricing—one for preferred pharmacies and one for standard pharmacies. Using a preferred pharmacy or mail-order will usually get you the lowest copays possible on your plan.

How Do the Four Phases Work?

You reach each phase only when you have spent enough to complete the prior phase. Your first phase is the Part D deductible.

Phase 1: Deductible

Medicare itself sets the maximum drug deductible annually, and most plans will incorporate that maximum deductible. They are not allowed to charge a higher deductible.

However, some plans may choose to offer a lower deductible to attract you to their plan, but be careful. If you look closely, you'll notice that those plans typically have higher premiums and higher copays for not charging the maximum deductible. In 2021, the maximum deductible is $445. If you choose a plan that incorporates the full deductible, that's what you can expect to spend before your benefits kick in.

Each time you fill a prescription, you'll pay the drug's full price. This amount will be applied toward your deductible until the plan calculates that you have spent $445 out of pocket. For example, let's say you fill a prescription for a tier 3 drug while you are still in your deductible phase. If the retail price for that drug is $70, then that's what you'll pay. The plan subtracts $70 from $445, and now you only have $375 left to meet your deductible.

You may also see that some plans apply the deductible only to the higher tiers. If you enroll in one of these plans and only take drugs in the lower tiers, you may not incur any deductible spending. For example, suppose your plan has a $445 deductible for tiers 3, 4, and 5 only. In that case, you can fill drugs in tiers 1 and 2 without incurring the deductible. Instead, you'll just pay your copay when you fill a tier 1 or 2 medication right from Day 1 of your plan.

Using our same tier list example from before, here's how the plan might look if it applies the deductible only to the higher tiers:

TIERS	INITIAL COVERAGE	COVERAGE GAP	CATASTROPHIC COVERAGE
Preferred Generic	$1.00 copay (ded. waived)	**Generic drugs:**	**Generic drugs:**
Generic	$7.00 copay (ded. waived)	25%	$3.70 copay or 5% (whichever costs more)
Preferred Brand	$42.00 copay	**Brand-name drugs:**	**Brand-name drugs:**
Non-Preferred Drug	35%	25%	$9.20 copay or 5% (whichever costs more)
Specialty Tier	25%		

Figure 4-3. Deductible Waived on Lower Tiers.

Once you have satisfied the plan's deductible, you move on to Phase 2, the initial coverage phase.

Phase 2: Initial Coverage

Once you enter the initial coverage phase, you will pay the specific copay or coinsurance for the tier in which that drug falls. You will pay this whenever you pick up the medication (or order it through a mail-order pharmacy). For example, if your plan specifies that tier 1 drugs have a $1 copay, you'll pay $1 whenever you pick up your medication. If it specifies that the copay for that tier is $5, you'll pay no more than $5.

Every time you fill a medication, your plan tracks the total cost of that medication. It uses your spending and your plan's spending to determine if and when you reach the initial coverage limit and fall into the coverage gap (commonly referred to as the "donut hole"). In 2021, you'll pay your regular drug copays until you reach the initial coverage limit, which occurs at $4,130 in total drug costs (between you, the manufacturer, and your plan). Of course, not everyone will hit this limit. Many people take inexpensive maintenance medications, so their annual drug cost tally is far lower than $4,130. For those who DO reach it, the next phase is the coverage gap.

Phase 3: Coverage Gap ("Donut Hole")

The coverage gap is the phase of your drug plan during which there is a temporary limit on what the plan will pay toward your covered medications. Beneficiaries used to dread the coverage gap, but thanks to the ACA legislation, your cost in the gap has gradually decreased over the last several years.

In 2006, when beneficiaries reached the coverage gap, they usually paid 100% of the cost of their medications until they hit the catastrophic coverage phase. It was brutal.

When you enter the gap today, the most you will pay is 25% of a covered drug's cost.

There is one caveat I want to mention here. Sometimes drug plans voluntarily choose to charge you a lower copay for drugs while you are in the initial coverage phase. When you reach the gap, they switch to charging you the full 25% drug cost while you are in the gap. In other words, they charge you less than 25% during initial coverage, which often benefits you.

However, if you reach the gap, you may then see an increase in your out-of-pocket spending for that same medication. While paying more isn't fun, it's certainly better than being charged that higher amount during both phases. Keep in mind that the Part D plan is often getting these drugs at a significant discount on retail prices, but when you reach the coverage gap, they can still charge you 25% of the actual drug cost. You will continue paying that until your total drug costs reach $6,550 for the year 2021. Then the catastrophic phase kicks in. It's a blessed relief for the small percentage of people who unfortunately get there.

Figure 4-4. The Donut Hole.

Phase 4: Catastrophic Coverage

When you reach the catastrophic coverage phase of your drug plan, your plan pays most of the cost of your covered medications for the rest of the year. As I stated earlier, catastrophic coverage is an essential piece of what you are buying when you enroll in Part D.

It's nice to have only a small or even zero copay for drugs in the earlier phases. However, the catastrophic coverage protects you from the kind of drug spending that would put you in the poor house. The catastrophic coverage phase kicks in when your True Out-of-Pocket (TrOOP) spending reaches the limit set by Medicare for the current year. In 2021, the TrOOP is $6,550. This is not a hard cap, but rather a limit at which your drug costs decrease significantly.

Most of the expenses that you pay for covered Part D medications count toward the TrOOP. Your deductible spending, your drug cost-sharing for covered formulary medications, and your coverage gap expenses all count toward this limit.

Your monthly premiums do NOT count toward the TrOOP. Neither do any expenses that you incur toward medications not covered in the formulary.

Once you have reached the TrOOP, your plan will cover about 95% of your covered drug costs for the rest of that calendar year. You will pay a small copay or no more than 5% of the drug's cost, whichever is greater. These parameters apply whether you get your coverage from a standalone Part D plan or one that lives inside a Medicare Advantage plan. They also change each year as Medicare adjusts the amount of the deductible and the limits at which you progress to each new phase.

We update these limits on our website every year, and you can find them here along with a video where I break down how Medicare Part D works. Type this URL into your internet browser to see this year's limits: https://boomerbenefits.link/part-d-costs

All Drug Plans Have Minimum Standards

Part D companies must follow Medicare's rules and guidelines for Part D plans when designing their coverage and drug formulary.

Even an inexpensive drug plan has minimum requirements that insurance companies must build into the coverage. For example, Medicare requires that each Part D drug plan offer at least two drugs in each therapeutic class. You may develop a new health condition in the middle of the year. Your doctor needs to have some medication choices that he or she can prescribe to you that are covered by your plan.

Part D plans must also cover all or substantially all drugs in six critical categories: antidepressants, antipsychotics, anticonvulsants, immunosuppressants, anticancer medications, and HIV/AIDS drugs. You will find these drugs in the formulary for every Part D drug plan.

What Drugs Fall outside of Part D?

Likewise, there are certain classes of medications that Medicare **does not** require drug plan carriers to offer in their formularies. These include:

- Barbiturates—sedatives or other drugs that depress the central nervous system

- Benzodiazepines—commonly prescribed for insomnia or anxiety
- Fertility or erectile dysfunction medications
- Medications for cosmetic reasons such as hair growth
- Drugs for weight loss, weight gain, or anorexia
- Prescription-strength vitamins and minerals
- Cough syrups or other meds that treat cold symptoms

Part D plans usually do not cover compounded medications either. If you take a dosage that is different from the standard dosage and requires compounding, you will typically pay the retail price for that medication.

You may occasionally find a Part D drug plan carrier that *chooses to offer* one of these drugs. However, that is the carrier's decision to do so. Each year, when the insurance carrier refiles the drug plan with Medicare, it can remove the medication from the formulary for the next year if they no longer wish to cover it.

Conditional Approval

Part D plans can apply several conditions for using specific medications. These conditions affect whether you can obtain the drug and how much of it you can get each time you refill a prescription. The insurance carriers call these "utilization management tools," but you might think of these as conditions for approval.

Quantity Limits

This condition is probably the easiest one to understand. A quantity limit is a restriction set by the Medicare drug plan, limiting how much of a medication it will cover over a period of time.

For example, you might find that your plan limits one of your pain medication to 60 pills per month.

Suppose your doctor prescribes more than the plan's quantity limit. In that case, the insurance company will request him to fill out a drug exception form explaining why more is needed. When the plan approves the request, your pharmacy can then fill the prescription. If the insurance company denies the exception request, the pharmacy won't fill more than the quantity limit allows.

You, of course, can appeal decisions when you disagree. We won't go into the appeal processes here in this book. However, you can find information about them in your drug plan's "Summary of Benefits." There is also information about appeals and grievances on the Boomer Benefits website. We've learned a great deal about helping our policyholders with them over the years.

We see many quantity limits come into play with addictive medications. If you take pain medication, check your drug formulary to learn what quantity limits might apply.

Prior Authorization

Some medications require your doctor to provide additional paperwork. A *prior authorization requirement* means that you or your doctor must obtain plan approval before a pharmacy is allowed to dispense your medication.

The insurance company may ask for proof that the prescription is medically necessary before they will cover it. This rule usually affects medications that are expensive or very potent. The doctor must show why this specific medication is required for you and why he or she considers less expensive alternative drug options to be harmful or ineffective.

Step Therapy

Step Therapy is when the plan will require you to try a lower-priced medication before it steps up to cover a more expensive medication. Though the plan lists the more expensive drug on its formulary, it will require you to try cheaper alternative medications that treat the same condition first. If the alternative medicine works, both you and the insurance company save money.

If it doesn't, your doctor can file an exception with your carrier to request coverage for the first medication prescribed. Your doctor will have to explain why you need the more expensive medicine when less costly alternatives are available. Often this requires that he or she show documentation that you have already tried alternatives that were not effective. Our Client Service Team helps our clients with many drug exception requests related to step therapy. It's been our experience that presenting proper documentation of how the past usage of certain drugs was not effective helps get exceptions approved.

How Do You Choose a Part D Drug Plan?

Most states have 20 or more drug plans. A Medicare insurance agent can help you run a Part D analysis to find the plans that will be the most cost-effective for you. Medicare also offers a free account to every Medicare beneficiary called MyMedicare.gov. It provides a free "Medicare Plan Finder Tool" to help you select the drug plan in your state that gives you the lowest annual out-of-pocket costs. You enter your medications into the Plan Finder Tool, including the dosage and frequency at which you take these medications. The Plan Finder will save this medication list for you inside your portal so that you can easily update it each fall when it comes time to shop for next year's Part D drug plan.

You can also choose your favorite pharmacies, including mail-order pharmacies, and ask to see plans that give you the best pricing at those pharmacies.

Once you have entered your medications, the Plan Finder Tool will display a list of Part D drug plans offered in your area. You can sort them by your "lowest drug + premium cost" to find and enroll in the plan that will cover your medications at the *lowest overall annual cost.*

Don't just enroll in the cheapest drug plan without doing your research. That plan may not include your medications in its formulary. Instead, *sort for the lowest drug + premium cost.* You will get a list of plans offering the lowest TOTAL out-of-pocket costs with all things considered: premiums, deductibles, and copays for your medications combined.

Also, don't forget to include any Part D IRMAA that you may owe. As we covered earlier, people with higher incomes who pay an IRMAA for Part B will also pay one for Part D. This may factor into your decision about which plans are affordable for you.

Our agency produces an annual video for our Part D policy-holders. It walks them through how to review their drug plan options inside their MyMedicare.gov portal. We also provide phone support for our clients as they analyze their choices.

✱ *Income Related Monthly adjustment Amount*

If you decide to tackle this on your own, just remember that Medicare also offers free help to analyze your drug options. You can reach them at 1-800-MEDICARE.

Managing Part D

With so many different phases and conditions for approval, Part D can quickly get confusing. Your plan will mail out the Explanation of Benefits (EOB) statements that show what you paid versus what the plan paid. You'll see your progress toward the various phase limits as well.

> **BOOMER BENEFITS PRO TIP:** Most Part D insurance companies also have their own member websites. You can use the data from your Member ID card to register for an online account. When you log in, you'll be able to find all sorts of great data about how much you have spent and how much your plan has covered. Accessing this data in your portal is often speedier than waiting for the EOB statement in the mail.

Finally, if you have low income, you may qualify for a Low-Income Subsidy (LIS) to help you pay for your Part D premiums, deductibles, and copays. You can learn more and see if you qualify here: https://www.ssa.gov/benefits/medicare/prescriptionhelp/

Sometimes, you can get cheaper generics through a discount card. When you fill prescriptions this way, they fall outside of Part D altogether. Then they don't use up any of the dollars left in your initial coverage phase before you reach the gap.

Now that you have dipped your toe into the water concerning Part D, let me share another common mistake with you surrounding Part D that we continually warn our own clients about at the time of enrollment, which is the subject of the next chapter.

> **BOOMER BENEFITS PRO TIP:** Check out the popular GoodRX drug discount program. Present both cards at the pharmacy and ask your pharmacist to tell you which one will give you the lowest copay. Discount programs like this one are also helpful for finding discounts on medications that fall outside of Part D. Learn more at https://www.goodrx.com/

Key Takeaways

Medicare Part D is the newest part of Medicare. It provides optional coverage through private insurance companies to help with the cost of your prescription medications. Here are the important points to remember:

- You can enroll in a Part D plan during your IEP. Thereafter, enrollment is limited to the AEP in the fall unless you have a circumstance that qualifies you for a Special Enrollment Period. *a mo*
- If you don't enroll and don't have other creditable coverage, you will accumulate a late penalty. Once you enroll, you will pay this penalty for as long as you remain enrolled in Part D.
- There are two ways to enroll in Part D. You can purchase

a standalone Part D drug plan or enroll in a Medicare Advantage plan that includes Part D.

- *Failing to enroll in Part D means you don't have any prescription coverage, which could leave you unable to pay for medications if you get sick. This is why you shouldn't skip Part D.*

- Part D plans have four phases that govern how much you will pay for medications while in that phase. These are the deductible, initial coverage, the coverage gap, and catastrophic coverage.

- The limits for each phase are set by Medicare each year.

- When you reach the catastrophic coverage phase of your drug plan, your plan pays most of the cost of your covered medications for the rest of the year.

- All Part D companies can employ utilization management tools to assess whether a medication is appropriate as prescribed before the company covers it.

- Using your personal MyMedicare.gov portal is the best way to search for the most cost-effective drug plan for your specific medications.

Chapter 5

MEDICARE MISTAKE #5:

Failing to Keep and Submit Proof of Your Creditable Coverage

If you work past 65 and delay enrollment into Part D because you have employer coverage, you will have two months to enroll in Medicare Part D coverage from your last day of work at your former employer.

Your former health insurance company will send you a vital piece of mail once your employer cancels your coverage due to your retirement. This letter is worth its weight in gold to Medicare beneficiaries, so keep an eye out for it.

The Certificate of Creditable Coverage

After your last day of work, your employer will notify your health insurance provider that you are no longer working there. This notification will trigger the insurance company to mail you a document called a **certificate of creditable coverage.**

Watch your mail carefully for it. You need to save this letter that shows proof of creditable coverage wherever you keep your important files and documents. More importantly, you need to know what to do with the information in this letter when you sign up for Part D.

Medicare Mistake #5: Failing to Keep and Submit Proof of Your Creditable Coverage

Here's the scenario: You did not enroll in Part D at 65 because you were still working, and your employer coverage covers your medications. Now you have just retired and have left your employer plan. You enroll in a Part D plan. The Part D insurer will immediately send you a Notice of Late-Enrollment Penalty in the mail that requires your prompt response.

The notice will tell you that Medicare's records show that you may owe this penalty. It explains what the late-enrollment penalty is. It also states that you can avoid the penalty if you can present proof of your creditable coverage since you turned 65. Enclosed with this notice, you will find a form where you can provide a declaration of prior prescription drug coverage. **Chances are that no one else will tell you anything about this Notice of Late-Enrollment Penalty (LEP), so bookmark this chapter!**

This notice often gets tossed out by unsuspecting Medicare

beneficiaries who don't realize they need to respond to it in a very short time frame. To respond, you will need the dates of your prior coverage that are *listed on your creditable coverage letter* from your employer.

- Fill out the declaration form with your dates of creditable coverage.
- Sign and return the form in the envelope provided by your Part D insurance company.

OR

- Call the Part D company at the hotline number provided in the notice. Give them your dates of creditable coverage by phone on a recorded line.

BOOMER BENEFITS PRO TIP: Our Client Service Team Manager here at Boomer Benefits advises that you do both. First, call the 1-800 number listed on the form. Give them a verbal attestation of the dates of your creditable coverage. Second, as a backup, fill out the notice with the dates of your creditable coverage and mail it back to the Part D insurance company in the envelope provided. She recommends this because we have seen some instances in which the company representative takes your recorded information by phone and fails to hit the submit button at the end of the call. The recording never gets submitted. Now you get a late penalty even though you DID call them with the info.

If you both call them and fill out the form with the same information and return it to the Part D company, you've gone the extra mile. It ensures that they get this information one way or another. It's better to be safe than sorry. Then, put your letter of creditable coverage away in a safe place where you can find it again.

The insurance company may ask for a copy of your creditable coverage letter. If you don't save it, you have to call your old insurance company to ask that they send a new one. For some reason, it's often difficult to get them to do this. Don't ask me why; it should be simple enough for them to send another. However, it isn't simple. We often see new Medicare beneficiaries going around and around with their former insurance company trying to obtain a new copy.

To recap this, I want you to notice that there are two parts to what I'm telling you in this short chapter:

1. *Save your certificate of creditable coverage in a safe place.*
2. *Be on the lookout for the Notice of Late-Enrollment Penalty from your new Part D carrier asking for creditable coverage dates.*

I've provided sample copies of the certificate of creditable coverage and the late-enrollment penalty notice at the end of this chapter (Exhibits 1-3). This will give you an idea of what they look like.

Why Do People Miss the Notice of Late Penalty?

Many people throw the creditable coverage certificate away because they simply don't recognize its significance. Other people *do* keep the creditable coverage letter but completely miss the Part D company's potential penalty notice. It is easy to overlook because the Part D company will mail out a whole bunch of other stuff to you around the same time: proof of enrollment, ID cards, an "Evidence of Coverage" booklet, and so on. With so much Part D mail coming your way, it's easy to miss the letter asking you to attest to the dates you were covered.

If you miss these steps, the Part D company is required by Medicare to assess the late penalty. You'll find yourself forced to pay a penalty that you don't owe. You can appeal this decision through Medicare's contractor, Maximus. However, it often takes months to resolve. You must continue to pay the penalty until Maximus has made a decision regarding your appeal. If you don't pay it, they can cancel your drug coverage.

If you enrolled in your policies through Boomer Benefits, our Client Service Team will provide you free help you with this appeal because it's such a tedious process. However, if you enrolled on your own directly with an insurance company, you will need to handle that appeal process yourself. It's a beast. Save your creditable coverage letter instead, and complete and return the Notice of Late-Enrollment Penalty form promptly to avoid an appeal altogether.

FAQ: What if I am over 65 and never receive a Notice of Late Penalty from my new Part D carrier?

Answer: Call your Part D carrier no later than four weeks from your policy effective date to provide them your proof of creditable coverage in a verbal attestation – the earlier, the better.

Key Takeaways

I hope that I have helped you avoid this appeal process altogether by making you aware of what the insurance company expects you to do. It is much easier to save your creditable coverage letter in the first place. You'll be ready to respond promptly to the notice that the Part D company mails out to you.

Here are the points to remember for this chapter:

- If you work past 65 and delay enrollment into Part D because you have employer coverage, you will have two months from the time your insurance ends to enroll in Medicare Part D.
- Failing to enroll in Part D during this window may result in a Part D late penalty.
- Your former insurance company will send you a letter of creditable coverage in the mail, usually within two weeks of your last day worked.
- Save your certificate of creditable coverage in a safe place.
- Use the information provided on the creditable coverage letter to provide your new Part D insurance company the information it requests in the Notice of Late-enrollment Penalty.

Now you know what mistakes to avoid related to Part D. Let's begin to look at your options for supplemental coverage if you don't have employer-funder retiree or government coverage.

Exhibit 5-1.

Sample Notice of Late-Enrollment

Department of Health and Human Services
Center for Medicare and Medicaid Services

Jane C Doe
5555 First Avenue
Somewhere, TX 75067

Member Number 89017892-98

August 16, 2020

Dear Jane,

Medicare records show that you may owe a Late Enrollment Penalty (LEP) on your monthly ABCInsurance Medicare RX (PDP) premiums.

What is an LEP?

The LEP is a penalty that Medicare applies to your monthly prescription drug plan premiums. If you went at least 63 days without creditable prescription drug coverage that met the minimum standards set by Medicare, then a penalty is added. It appears that you did not have coverage from 08/01/2016 to 07/31/2020.

How can I avoid the penalty?

To avoid the penalty, you must notify us that you did have prescription drug coverage during the dates listed above. You can notify us by contacting us no later than **September 15, 2020.**

- By mail: Complete the form we have enclosed and return it to ABCInsurance MedicareRX
- By telephone: call our customer service team at 1-888-555-5555, TTY 711, 9am – 9pm CST, 7 days per week.

What happens if fail to respond by the deadline?

Medicare will decide that you owe the penalty and it will be added to your monthly drug plan premium each month for as long as you remain enrolled in Part D drug coverage.

Note: For additional information, see the Frequently Asked Questions letter that we have included in this letter.

Exhibit 5-2.

Penalty for Part D

Declaration of Prior Prescription Drug Coverage

Please complete the information below to share with us when you believe you had creditable prescription drug coverage that meets Medicare's minimum standards. You can mark any of the boxes that are true for you.

ABCInsurance Medicare RX (PDP) Member Number: 89017892-98

Type of creditable coverage	Dates of Coverage:	
	Start Date	**End Date**
__Employer or Union or Federal Employee Health Benefits	_____	_____
__Medicaid or a similar plan offered in my state	_____	_____
__Veterans Affairs	_____	_____
__TRICARE or other military coverage	_____	_____
__A Retiree Medicare policy with drug coverage	_____	_____
__Indian Health Service, a Tribe or Tribal organization	_____	_____
__ PACE (Program of All-Inclusive Care for the Elderly)	_____	_____
__Other Creditable Coverage	_____	_____
__ I had Extra Help with Part D from Medicare	_____	_____

Exhibit 5-3.

Sample Certificate of Creditable Coverage

Certificate of Creditable Coverage Letter

Jane C Doe
5555 First Avenue
Somewhere, TX 75067

August 5, 2020

Identification Number of Covered Member: ZBQ09261830

Dear Mrs. Doe:

The Health Insurance Portability and Accountability Act of 1996 (HIPAA) requires a group health plan to provide a certificate of creditable coverage to members whose coverage under the health plan is ending. The purpose of this creditable coverage letter is to give such person a credit toward the satisfaction of waiting periods a new health insurance plan may have for any pre-existing conditions. Below is your certificate of creditable coverage:

CERTIFICATE OF CREDITABLE COVERAGE

Date of Certificate Issuance: August 5, 2020

Name of Member to whom this certificate applies: Jane C Doe

ID Number of Member: ZBQ09261830

Name of the Group Health Plan: XYZ Medical Plan

Date Coverage Began: 02/01/2009

Date Coverage Ended: 07/31/2020

Name, address and phone number of plan administrator or issuer responsible for providing this certificate:

ABC Allied Insurance
1234 Broadway St.
Dallas, TX 75028

Have questions about this notice? You call us at 1-888-555-5555 for help or more information.

Part 4

MAJOR DECISION:

Which Route Should You Choose to Go with Medicare?

Chapter
6

MEDICARE MISTAKE #6:

Assuming Preexisting Conditions Don't Matter

Before I describe Mistake #6, I need to set the stage a bit by sharing my perspective. The reason so many people make bad choices when it comes to supplemental coverage is that they have too many options.

Just last month in our private Facebook group, where Medicare beneficiaries can ask us their questions, we took a poll. We asked our group members to tell us what they wish they had understood about Medicare before they enrolled.

My favorite answer was from John A.: "That you need a master's degree in Health Planning before you can choose a plan."

Another member replied to his comment: "I *have* a master's

degree, and still this is all just painful and overwhelming and shouldn't be."

Over the years, we have heard similar comments from thousands of beneficiaries.

The Problem of too many Choices

I've often wondered why the government doesn't do a better job of preparing people for Medicare. After all, during your working years, your employers selected your medical plans for you. Sure, you may have had one or two choices. Maybe your employer gave you a choice between a plan with a PPO (Preferred Provider Organization) network or a less expensive plan with an HMO (Health Maintenance Organization) network, or perhaps between two similar health plans but one with a high deductible and one with a low deductible.

Most people know that PPO networks generally allow for some coverage outside the network at a higher cost. HMO plans are typically closed networks and may have little to no coverage outside the network except in emergencies.

But there's nothing in your lifetime of using health insurance to prepare you for the overwhelming number of choices you must sort through when you finally become eligible for Medicare. It's the reason that so many beneficiaries get hopelessly confused. To simplify things for you, I'm going to boil down all the dozens of plan options into **just two main routes** you can go. You can choose either:

1. a Medigap plan with a standalone Part D drug plan, or
2. a Medicare Advantage plan (that may include Part D).

Determining which one is right for you is one of the essential tasks that you will face regarding Medicare. It is not a decision to make lightly, either. You should become familiar with each route before choosing because *you can't have both*. As I go over these two routes, you'll soon recognize that what makes the most sense for someone in stellar health is not the same for someone with many medical problems. In this chapter, we discuss the first route, Medigap plans. We will discuss Medicare Advantage plans in the next chapter.

Costs are also a significant concern for many people when choosing between Original Medicare + Medigap or a Medicare Advantage plan. Besides the premiums that you pay for each type of coverage, there are back-end costs that you must consider as you are deciding which route to go. Other issues like prescription drug coverage and provider networks will also factor into your choice. *Though there are several things to consider, remember that you are ultimately choosing between only two different ways to get your benefits.*

There's something else you must know. Preexisting conditions will not affect your ability to get Original Medicare itself. However, they CAN affect your ability to get a Medigap plan outside of a special Medigap Open Enrollment Period (Medigap OEP) in many states. Medical *underwriting* will apply in most states if you miss this window. *Underwriting* is the process by which an insurance company assesses the financial risk to them if they provide you with health insurance coverage.

When underwriting, the Medigap company could decline to issue you a policy due to *preexisting health conditions*. Some examples of preexisting health conditions that might result in a denial of coverage include heart disease, diabetes, cancer, lung disorders like chronic obstructive pulmonary disease, and auto-immune disorders. Each company has its own underwriting guidelines, so decisions will vary.

Medicare Mistake #6: Assuming Preexisting Conditions Don't Matter

While preexisting conditions don't matter for getting Medicare itself, they *do matter* when it comes to supplemental coverage.

Everyone gets a one-time opportunity to buy a Medigap plan without any health questions asked. Around here, we call this the Golden Ticket, and I'll explain it in much more detail later in this chapter.

What's essential for you to know is that many Medicare beneficiaries miss this one-time opportunity and don't realize it until their chance has passed. Why? Because they have mistaken beliefs about what they can and can't do during Medicare's various enrollment periods. So why would so many beneficiaries make such a grave mistake? They assume that the "no under-writing" provision of the 2010 Patient Protection and Affordable Care Act (PPACA) legislation pertains to Medigap plans.

It doesn't.

The Patient Protection and Affordable Care Act

PPACA, also known as the Obamacare legislation, changed the qualifications that enable Americans to buy individual health insurance coverage. Per the healthcare.gov website, it provides "numerous rights and protections that make health coverage fairer and easier to understand."

PPACA included many provisions affecting Medicare. For example, it improved some of Medicare's preventive care benefits and began slowly closing the Medicare Part D donut hole. It also created the Health Insurance Marketplace (or Exchange) to make it easy for people under 65 without health coverage to evaluate and enroll in a health plan. Most important, it requires insurers in the under-65 market to cover people with preexisting health conditions without charging more or turning them away.

However, Medicare is not part of the Health Insurance Exchange. Therefore, this provision of PPACA does not apply to people who have Medicare itself and now want to buy optional Medigap coverage. **In other words, PPACA does not allow you to wait until you get sick to sign up for a Medigap plan.**

Many Medicare beneficiaries mistakenly assume they can skip the health questions on a Medigap application because of the PPACA legislation. It's a rude awakening when they learn this just isn't the case.

Medicare and Preexisting Conditions

While this might first feel unfair, it really isn't because you already get *access to Medicare itself* without any health questions.

Medicare is your primary health insurance coverage. That coverage is provided to you at age 65 without any preexisting condition limitations or rate-ups. You are already getting the same "free pass" into Original Medicare that PPACA provides to people under 65.

Medigap plans, on the other hand, are not primary coverage. They are optional, voluntary, private supplemental health insurance coverage that you can choose to purchase or not. Therefore, Medigap carriers in most states do not have to accept you for coverage unless you are applying during your one-time Medigap OEP or unless you otherwise qualify for a Guaranteed Issue Period, which only applies in certain circumstances. (There are a few exceptions that I go over in the following sections.)

FAQ: Why is it so important that people don't miss their opportunity to get a Medigap plan with no health questions asked?

Answer: The coverage level you get when combining Original Medicare with a Medigap plan is quite comprehensive. It's the "Cadillac Coverage" when it comes to supplemental insurance. Let's take a look at the details for Original Medicare + a Medigap plan.

Option 1: Original Medicare + Medigap

Medigap plans have been around since the 1960s when President Lyndon Johnson first signed Medicare into law. They are private policies that pay after Medicare. They help pay your portion of Medicare cost-sharing expenses. That means they are supplementing what Medicare already pays toward your covered Parts A and B services.

For example, you can enroll in a Medigap plan that will pay your Part A hospital deductible AND your 20% Part B coinsurance. Then you won't have to pay these things out of your pocket.

Except for some foreign travel benefits in a couple of plans, Medigap plans generally *do not* cover things that fall outside of Medicare, like hearing aids or cosmetic services. However, when it comes to medically necessary services, Medigap plans provide excellent coverage.

When you have Medicare and a Medigap plan, Medicare is the party that determines whether any claim is covered or isn't covered. If Medicare approves a claim, it will pay its share and then send the remainder on to your Medigap company, which must also then pay its share. The Medigap plan pays for the things that otherwise you would have had to pay, such as the previously mentioned deductibles and coinsurance. Fortunately, Medicare does approve the vast majority of claims it receives. In 2018 alone, it paid out $731 billion.

When reviewing the two routes that you can take to defray your potential Medicare spending, you'll find that Medigap plans usually have higher premiums than Medicare Advantage plans. However, you'll have less spending later because the Medigap plan picks up most of your back-end expenses. Individuals who choose Original Medicare and a Medigap plan often do so because they want very predictable expenses. They are willing to pay a higher premium each month because they want peace of mind. Knowing exactly how much money they can expect to pay for a hospital stay or chronic illness is reassuring.

Here are some of the features you will find in a Medigap plan:

Freedom to Choose Your Providers

A Medigap plan allows you to choose your Medicare providers no matter where you happen to be in the country.

When you choose Medigap, you remain in the Original Medicare program with access to any of Medicare's providers.

Medicare offers more than 1 million providers nationwide, and about 93% of physicians accept Original Medicare. This kind of flexibility and freedom of choice is vital to many people. It is especially appealing if you frequently travel in the United States. We have quite a few clients who live the snowbird lifestyle, going to warmer states in the winter and returning north for the summers. They can use their Medigap coverage to see doctors in both places.

No Referrals Necessary

*With a Medigap plan, your coverage will be accepted by any provider who accepts Medicare **regardless of which insurance company you choose for your Medigap coverage.***

There are no networks to hassle with and no requirement that you must choose a primary care physician (PCP). If you want to see a dermatologist, you can use Medicare's online directory of providers to find one in your area. You won't need a referral from PCP. This becomes especially important if you need treatment for something life-threatening. For example, here in Texas, we have M.D. Anderson in Houston, which is arguably one of the nation's best cancer treatment centers. If you develop cancer and want to get your treatment at M.D. Anderson, you can. You don't have to check in with your PCP or secure any paperwork.

Our team frequently helps new clients decide between a Medigap plan or a Medicare Advantage plan. We often find that a hospital or doctor's nonparticipation in Medicare Advantage plans makes a choice very simple. If your preferred doctors and hospitals do not participate in any of the Medicare

Advantage plans in your area, you'll want to stick with Original Medicare so you can continue seeing those doctors. You'll choose a Medigap plan *over* a Medicare Advantage plan in this scenario.

Higher Premiums but Predictable Back-End Spending

I mentioned that Medigap plans generally have higher premiums than Medicare Advantage plans. That's because Medigap plans offer you the most freedom and flexibility in getting your medical services. They also provide reassurance that you will owe little to nothing at the time of your care, depending on which Medigap plan you choose.

Ability to Choose the Best Drug Coverage for You

Medigap plans were created in the 1960s long before Part D was created and then rolled out in 2006. They helped to fill in the gaps in Original Medicare as it was established in 1965 before drug coverage became a part of Medicare.

Therefore, Medigap plans do not include Part D.

> Thomas has a chronic health condition, which requires him to see a specialist every few weeks. He also likes to travel here in the United States, frequently heading to Oklahoma from his home in Texas to see his grandchildren, sometimes staying for weeks. Thomas opts for a Medigap plan so that he can seek medical treatment in both Oklahoma and Texas.

If you elect to stay with Original Medicare and enroll in a Medigap plan, you will also need to enroll in a standalone Part D plan if you want coverage for outpatient medications. The benefit here is that you can customize your Part D coverage. You do so by simply choosing the individual Part D drug plan that offers you the best prices for your specific medications. You aren't stuck with the drug formulary that has been lumped into your primary coverage like you would be with a Medicare Advantage plan.

Similarly, Medigap plans do not cover routine vision, dental, and hearing costs. Fortunately, many insurance companies offer affordable standalone coverage to help with these costs. You can choose from inexpensive discount plans to more costly fully insured coverage that will pay for a portion of your actual expenses.

No Claims Paperwork

Medicare processes many millions of claims each year. You'll be happy to know that your involvement in that will be minimal, both with Medicare itself and with your Medigap company.

FAQ: Will I need to file claims with my Medigap company?

Answer: Fortunately, no. Participating Medicare providers will typically file Medicare claims for covered supplies and services that you receive.

Even if your provider doesn't bill Medicare, most Medigap companies also have crossover filing with Medicare. Medicare will transfer the paid claims data to the Medigap company so that it can pay its share. Anytime that Medicare approves a claim and pays its share, your Medigap plan must also pay its share. As a last resort, you can file your own claim by submitting a Patient's Request for Medical Payment (CMS-1490S).

Guaranteed Renewability

Medigap plans are guaranteed renewable. They cannot drop you or change your coverage if you develop a new health condition. The only reason they will cancel you is if you fail to pay your premiums.

Consistent Benefits

Last but not least, the benefits inside most Medigap plans do not change from year to year as they do in Medicare Advantage plans. They remain consistent, making Medigap insurance the most predictable back-end coverage that you can buy. You do not have to review any upcoming benefit changes for the following year. These plans, therefore, require almost no homework in the way that Advantage plans do.

Eligibility for Medicare Supplements (Medigap)

To enroll in a Medigap plan, you must first enroll in both Medicare Parts A and B. Medigap plans cover only one person per policy. Your spouse must have his or her own policy. However, you may qualify for household discounts with some insurance companies.

Also, Medigap companies usually base their rates on your zip code. Some areas of the country are more expensive than others because the cost of health care in that area is high. (Your income does not affect your Medigap premiums as it does with Part B and D.)

Qualifying for a Medigap plan will often require you to pass a series of health questions. However, if you enroll in a Medigap plan during your Medigap OEP, you can skip the health questions.

Choosing a Medigap Policy

Realizing that too many choices cause confusion, Medicare standardized the Medigap plan choices into ten plans (plus high-deductible options for Plans F and G). Standardization helps beneficiaries compare apples to apples when choosing their policy.

Insurance companies who sell Medicare supplements do not have to offer all ten plans. However, the Medigap plans that a carrier *does* offer must cover the same benefits as policies of the same plan letter sold by another insurance company. For example, a Plan G from Insurance Company 1 must include the same benefits as a Plan G from Insurance Company 2. You can then compare prices, financial ratings, and rate increase histories to decide which insurance company's plan you want.

Figure 6-1 details the benefits covered by each different plan in most states. (Wisconsin, Minnesota, and Massachusetts plans have a different structure. Nonetheless, you can usually choose riders for your Medicare supplement in those states to make them similar in coverage to the more popular plans. If you live in one of these three states, visit our "States" page on our website to select your state and read about how Medigap plans work where you live: https://boomerbenefits.com/compare-medicare-plans-and-prices/states/.)

MEDIGAP BENEFITS CHART	Plan A	Plan B	Plan C	Plan D	Plan F	Plan G	Plan K	Plan L	Plan M	Plan N
Medicare Part A Coinsurance & Hospital Costs (Up to an additional 365 days after Medicare benefits are used)	100%	100%	100%	100%	100%	100%	100%	100%	100%	100%
Medicare Part B Coinsurance or Copayment	100%	100%	100%	100%	100%	100%	50%	75%	100%	***100%
Blood (First 3 Pints)	100%	100%	100%	100%	100%	100%	50%	75%	100%	100%
Part A Hospice Care Coinsurance or Copayment	100%	100%	100%	100%	100%	100%	50%	75%	100%	100%
Skilled Nursing Facility Coinsurance	X	X	100%	100%	100%	100%	50%	75%	100%	100%
Medicare Part A Deductible	X	100%	100%	100%	100%	100%	50%	75%	100%	100%
Medicare Part B Deductible	X	X	100%	X	100%	X	X	X	X	X
Medicare Part B Excess Charges	X	X	X	X	100%	100%	X	X	X	X
Foreign Travel Emergency (up to plan limits)	X	X	80%	80%	80%	80%	X	X	80%	80%
Out of Pocket Limit							$6,220	$3,110		

Figure 6-1. Medigap Benefits Chart showing the coverage
for Medigap plans available in most states.

You'll notice that plans start with Letter A and go through Letter N. The missing letters denote plans that have been retired.

The wide variety of plans allows you to customize the coverage to your needs and budget. You can choose a policy with just some coverage of the gaps in Medicare, such as Plan K. On the other hand, you could choose a policy that covers nearly all of the gaps, like Plan G. When I say "gaps," I'm referring to your Medicare deductibles, coinsurance, and copays.

Again, which Medigap plan is right for you is a personal choice based on how much cost-sharing you are willing to do. Most beneficiaries want a comprehensive plan that leaves them with almost nothing to pay as they receive services. Others prefer a plan in which they cover some of their deductibles and coinsurance to achieve lower premiums.

I should mention that *all* Medigap plans provide coverage for your Part A coinsurance and hospital fees for an additional 365 days beyond what Medicare provides. So even Medigap Plan A, the one with the least benefits, goes a considerable way toward protecting you from the things that might otherwise create financial strain. There is no right or wrong here. You just need to choose which plan makes the most sense *for you.*

Popular Plan Choices

For many years, Medigap Plans C and F were the most popular sellers. It's easy to see why—they cover the most benefits. These plans have often been referred to as "first-dollar coverage" because they cover both your Part A and B deductibles. Medigap Plans C and F would pick up at the first dollar whether you have an inpatient or outpatient procedure. These plans leave you with almost nothing out-of-pocket at the time of service.

However, as of 2020, new Medicare beneficiaries can no longer buy Plans C or F. Congress passed the Medicare Access and CHIP Reauthorization Act (MACRA) in 2015. It prohibits the sale of Medigap plans that cover the Part B deductible beginning in 2020. Beneficiaries who were eligible for Medicare before January 1, 2020, will always have the right to apply for Plan C or F, at least for as long as insurance companies still offer them. The legislation grandfathered these people. Newly eligible beneficiaries on or after January 1, 2020, *will not* have these two options.

> **FAQ:** Why can newly eligible Medicare beneficiaries no longer purchase Medigap Plan C or Plan F?
>
> **Answer:** Legislators want everyone to have some skin in the game. You might think twice about running to the doctor for a minor sniffle if you are responsible for paying your own Part B deductible. So now everyone must pay the Part B deductible out-of-pocket, regardless of which Medigap plan they choose (unless they qualify for Medicaid, which might pay it for them).

Wondering which plans then might be the most popular going forward? Enter Plan G and Plan N.

Medigap Plan G

The next most comprehensive plan behind Plan C or Plan F is Plan G.

Medigap Plan G covers your share of all Parts A and B covered services, except for the outpatient deductible. Medicare pays first. Then Plan G pays all the rest after you pay the annual deductible. Also, Plan G offers up to $50,000 in foreign travel emergency benefits.

Let's look at an example of how this coverage works in real life: Frank has diabetes. He enrolls in Plan G when he first becomes eligible for Medicare. He sees his primary care doctor once per year. However, he visits his endocrinologist several times a year to renew his prescriptions.

In January, he goes to his first doctor visit for the year. The specialist bills Medicare, which pays its 80% share of the bill except for the $203 outpatient deductible, which Frank must pay. His Medigap Plan G pays the rest. Frank's coverage even provides his lancets, test strips, and a new glucose meter at no charge to him. Medicare and his Medigap plan work together to pay 100% of the costs for these diabetes supplies.

Frank will owe absolutely nothing out-of-pocket for the rest of the year for covered Parts A and B services. He will only encounter copays for medications under his separate Part D prescription drug card. He doesn't have to worry about any more doctor copays. He won't pay for medically necessary lab work or imaging or even outpatient surgery. Plan G is an excellent Medigap fit for Frank in this respect.

Figure 6-2.

High-Deductible Plan G

Plan G has a new high-deductible option. When enrolled in a high-deductible Medigap policy, you pay all expenses for covered services until you meet the annual deductible. Then the plan begins to pay. High-deductible Medigap plans aren't all that popular because most people want fuller coverage of the gaps in Medicare. However, they offer lower premiums than other plans. In that respect, they may make sense for some beneficiaries who have significant cash on hand to handle unexpected medical spending.

With a high-deductible plan, Original Medicare will still pay its share of your medical services. After Medicare processes your claim and pays its share, you pay all costs until you reach the deductible of $2,370 (in 2021). Your spending toward that overall deductible could include your Part A and B deductibles and any other inpatient or outpatient spending. For example, you'll pay 20% of your Part B services until you satisfy the $2,370 deductible. After you meet the deductible, the plan will pay the same benefits as Plan G.

Although the lower monthly premiums on high-deductible plans can be appealing to some consumers, we frequently find that after they enroll in them, they don't like them. When your health providers are sending you a bill for 20% of every outpatient service you receive, it's easy to feel nickel-and-dimed. If little bills like that will annoy you, consider a fuller-coverage supplement. That said, I do think they have their place. If you have other options for medical care like VA benefits, then a high-deductible Plan G as a backup to your Medicare can work well.

Medigap Plan N

Medigap Plan N typically has lower premiums than Plan G because you'll cover a bit more yourself.

In addition to paying your own Part B deductible, you will pay copays of up to $20 for doctor visits and up to $50 for emergency visits. You will also pay excess charges if nonparticipating Medicare providers treat you. In contrast, Plan G covers excess charges for you.

Plan N has been popular since it first came onto the scene in 2010. It was designed for consumers who like paying a lower premium in exchange for taking on a few more of their outpatient costs.

Figure 6-3.

Here's a real-life example for Plan N using simple numbers for illustration purposes: Karen tells her agent that she visits the doctor only once or twice a year. She feels that a fuller coverage plan like Plan G isn't necessary due to her low medical usage. She is interested in Plan N because she can pay lower premiums while still enjoying full hospital coverage. Karen will pay the Part B deductible upon her first outpatient service of the year. She then spends a copayment of up to $20 when she sees her physicians during the rest of the year. She may pay an excess charge if her doctor is not a participating Medicare doctor.

Karen visits her podiatrist in the middle of the year after she has already met her deductible. Medicare's assigned rate for a visit to this foot specialist is $100. However, he does not accept Medicare's assigned rates. He can bill Karen for up to 15% beyond the approved rate for this visit, or a maximum of $15. Karen also owes her $20 copay. Her Medigap Plan N will pay the remainder of the approved charges.

Beneficiaries who choose Plan N can avoid excess charges by asking their medical providers if they accept Medicare's assigned rates. Doctors who accept Medicare's assigned rates agree not to charge excess charges. Occasionally, we do find that someone who enrolls in Plan N forgets to do this. They get small bills for a few dollars here and there and find it annoying. If you think you would feel the same, Plan G may fit you better.

Other Medigap Plans

It has been my experience at Boomer Benefits that Medicare beneficiaries rarely ask about the other Medigap plans. Indeed, the AHIP Center for Policy Research reported that in 2017:

- Less than 2% of individuals with Medigap had enrolled in Plan B.
- Less than 1% had enrolled in Plan A.
- Less than 1% had chosen Plans D and K.
- Less than 0.5% had chosen Plans L or M.

In my experience, this is because people living on fixed incomes prefer plans with more predictable coverage that leaves them with few surprises. Since so few beneficiaries show interest in these other plans, many Medigap carriers don't even bother offering them.

Medicare SELECT

A Medicare SELECT plan is a Medigap policy that limits your coverage to a network of hospitals (and in some cases, specific doctors). SELECT plans negotiate rates with these providers. The providers charge less for the services they provide to members. While this kind of policy may offer you slightly lower premiums, you should think carefully before purchasing one. Be aware of the following things:

- Many hospitals and treatment facilities will be out-of-network. Your Medicare SELECT policy will not cover the gaps in Medicare for treatment received at those places. You must receive care from providers in the network except for emergencies.
- SELECT policyholders may need to get referrals from their primary care doctor to see specialists or receive treatment at a network hospital.
- You should confirm that any SELECT policy you

choose has your preferred hospitals in its network before enrolling.

We rarely see people interested in Medicare SELECT policies. However, if they appeal to you, you can certainly check to see if any are available in your state.

Nonstandard States: Wisconsin, Minnesota, and Massachusetts

These three states prohibit the sale of the ten standardized Medigap plans. However, they do allow insurance companies to sell plans with very similar features. They usually come in the form of riders that you can add to basic coverage plans. For more specific details on the coverage in Wisconsin, Minnesota, and Massachusetts, visit our "States" pages for further information at https://boomerbenefits.com/compare-medicare-plans-and-prices/states/

Now, let's circle back to **the most important enrollment period** you'll face after enrolling in Medicare. This is one that you shouldn't miss if you want a Medigap plan but have preexisting conditions.

Your "Golden Ticket" to Buying a Medigap Plan

When you enroll in Medicare Part B, you will trigger a crucial one-time enrollment window to get a Medigap plan with no questions asked. If Medicare is going to be your primary coverage, *and you have health conditions*, you must not miss your Medigap Open Enrollment Period (Medigap OEP).

The Medigap OEP is a six-month period during which you

can enroll in any Medigap plan offered in your state without answering health questions. Companies that sell Medigap plans cannot turn you down for coverage when you apply during this period. They are not even allowed to ask you any health questions on the application during this period.

However, this period occurs only *once* for most people. It expires six months after your Part B effective date. *Then it is gone. It is not an annual enrollment period. It does not recur.* Don't miss it unless you have other creditable coverage for which you are delaying enrollment into Medicare. Failing to apply during this Medigap OEP can have lifelong consequences in the form of higher premiums and possibly limited coverage options.

Now, just because the Medigap OEP begins on your Part B effective date doesn't mean that you can't shop for your Medigap plan *before* that date. In other words, you *can* shop for your Medigap plan prior to that Part B effective date. Most people shop for their Medigap plan several months before turning 65. When you apply, you can specify that you want your Medigap policy effective date to match your Part B effective date. This qualifies as enrolling during your Medigap OEP, and there will be no health questions. *The main thing to keep in mind is that once your Medigap OEP expires, the Golden Ticket opportunity is gone.*

Medigap Open Enrollment Period (OEP)
6-month window that starts on your Part B effective date

Figure 6-4.

Facts about the Open Enrollment Period for Medigap

Here are the most important things for you to understand about your Medigap OEP:

- It only occurs once for *most* people. It is *not* annual.
- Your Part B effective date is the start of your personal Medigap OEP.
- It lasts for six months, and then it is gone.
- Once it's gone, you must answer health questions to get a Medigap plan or change your Medigap plan in most states.
- Exception: People on Medicare under age 65 (due to a disability) will get a rare second open enrollment for a Medigap plan later when they turn 65.

Matthew is turning 65 soon. His doctor recently diagnosed him with Parkinson's Disease. He decides that a Medigap Plan G would be in his best interest so that he doesn't have to pay any doctor copays for his frequent visits to specialists. He may not get another opportunity to obtain a Medigap plan. Just before he turns 65, he uses his Medigap OEP to enroll in a Plan G policy that will start alongside his Medicare on his Part B effective date.

Outside of this period, federal law does not require Medigap insurance carriers to accept you for coverage except in certain situations and states. Since Medigap policies are optional supplemental coverage, insurance carriers can accept or decline applications made after your one-time Medigap OEP ends. If you don't take advantage of your Medigap OEP, you could find later that you can't medically qualify for a policy. For this reason, it is often your best bet to enroll during your personal Medigap OEP.

What Happens if You Work past Age 65?

As we have already discussed, many people today work past age 65 and delay enrollment into Part B while still actively working. You might be one of them. Assuming you have creditable coverage from a large employer, you will probably enroll in just Part A as your secondary coverage while still working.

When you do retire, Medicare will give you a Special Enrollment Period (SEP) to enroll in Part B without a late penalty. Your Part B effective date then triggers that one-time Medigap OEP so that you won't miss out on it. By working with a broker ahead of time, you can enroll in Part B and a Medigap plan to take effect on the day after your employer coverage ends.

On the other hand, if you were working past 65 *for a small employer with less than 20 employees*, you may miss your one-time Medigap OEP because you must enroll in both Parts A and B when you turn 65. If you decide to use your employer coverage as secondary while you are still working, this causes a problem. Later, when you are ready to retire, your one-time Medigap OEP is long gone.

Now what?

Medicare has some guaranteed issue rules that will often protect you in this scenario.

Guaranteed Issue (GI) Periods

Medicare defines *guaranteed issue rights* as Medigap protections that you have in certain situations when insurance companies must offer you a Medigap policy. In these situations, the Medigap insurer must sell you a Medigap policy covering your preexisting health conditions. It cannot charge you more for a Medigap policy because of any health past or present health conditions.

There are *federal* guarantee issue protections available to you. Many *states* also have expanded qualifying events that allow you to buy a policy under guaranteed issue rules. You usually have a guaranteed issue right to buy a Medigap policy when you have existing creditable health coverage that changes or ends, such as due to retirement. If you have Medicare and have also maintained creditable employer health coverage, you will get a 63-day guaranteed issue window to buy certain policies. The 63-day GI window begins on the date your other coverage ends or on the date you get the notice telling you that your coverage is ending, whichever is later.

During a GI period, you can enroll with no health questions asked in:

- Medigap plans A, B, D, **F**, K, or L if you were first eligible for Medicare *before January 1, 2020.*
- Medigap plans A, B, D, **G**, K, or L if you were first eligible for Medicare *on or after January 1, 2020.*

Certain GI situations and certain insurance companies may also allow you to enroll in other Medigap plans than those I've listed here.

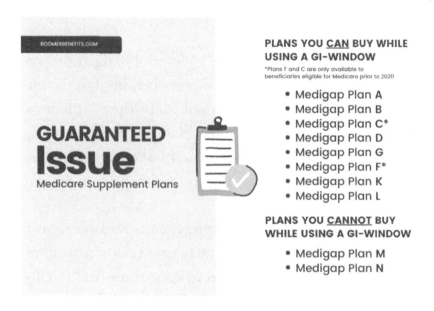

Figure 6-5. Medigap Plans that Qualify for GI.

You may also be given a GI right in other situations, such as:

- Your Medicare Advantage plan stops offering coverage in your area.
- You move out of your plan's service area and lose your Medicare Advantage coverage by doing so.
- You enroll in a Medicare Advantage plan for the first time. Within the first 12 months, you decide to switch back to Original Medicare.
- Your Medigap company goes out of business, causing you to lose your coverage (sounds scary, but I've never actually seen it happen).

These situations, and some others, may give you the right to choose a new Medigap policy without underwriting.

Your state may provide additional Medigap protections. In

some states, there are rules regarding whether you *voluntarily* lost your creditable coverage. These rules can affect your right to GI. Medicare insurance brokers like us are familiar with these rules and can guide you through the transition from employer coverage to Medigap coverage.

Exceptions to the One-Time Medigap OEP Rule

While most people get only ONE Medigap OEP in their lifetime, there are a couple of scenarios where more than one occurs.

Medigap Plans for People Under 65

Some people qualify for Medicare early due to disability or serious health conditions like End-Stage Renal Disease. You need to know that the rules surrounding Medigap options *are different for people under 65* than for people who are aging into Medicare at 65.

In some states, Medigap plans are not an option for people under 65. There are quite a few states that do not require Medigap insurance carriers to sell policies to people under 65. Advantage plans are usually the right choice for people under 65 in these states.

Other states require Medigap carriers to offer at least one Medigap plan to beneficiaries who are under 65. Sometimes that becomes the only plan that insurance companies will offer to people under 65. For example, in Texas, the law only requires carriers to offer Medigap Plan A to people under 65. What's worse is that the rates for Plan A for people under 65 can be ridiculously high because the claims are high for people on disability. Even when people under 65 do start with a Medigap plan, they eventually switch to a Medicare Advantage plan because they can't sustain the high annual rate increases. Ultimately, they can't afford the premiums.

Of course, someone in this situation usually does not want to stay on Plan A or a Medicare Advantage plan forever. Fortunately, Medicare gives them *a second 6-month Medigap OEP.* The law allows them a second chance at 65 to obtain fuller coverage when they can finally get that coverage at affordable prices and at the same rate as everyone else. They can use their second Medigap OEP to move from their current plan to a more comprehensive Medigap plan.

One of the reasons I like Medicare Advantage plans for people under 65 is that the rate is the same for everyone on the Advantage plan, regardless of age. Carriers can't increase the Medicare Advantage premium just because someone is under 65.

Beneficiaries Who Return to Work

Another exception occasionally occurs when someone already on Medicare Part B goes back to work and becomes eligible for large-employer coverage. People in this situation can choose their employer coverage over Medicare. They often disenroll from Part B and their Medigap plan because their new employer coverage already includes outpatient coverage.

Later, they retire and reenroll into Part B. That Part B effective date triggers a new 6-month Medigap OEP. Now they can once again set themselves up with supplemental coverage without worrying that the Medigap company will decline their application.

Chip becomes eligible for Medicare at age 63 after receiving 24 months of Social Security disability benefits. While he would prefer a Medigap plan, he learns that his state offers only Plan A for people under 65. The premiums are high at around $400/month. Therefore, he signs up for a Medicare Advantage plan for now since each Advantage plan offers the same premium to all enrollees, regardless of age. When he turns 65, he phones his agent, who helps him using a Special Enrollment Period to disenroll from his Advantage plan. He switches to a Medigap plan that will provide him fuller coverage. His premium for Plan G is just $150/month because he is aging into Medicare and not categorized as "under-65" any longer.

How Do You Qualify for a Medigap Plan?

There are three different ways that you can qualify for a Medigap plan. We've already covered two of them.

One is to apply during your 6-month Medigap OEP. I can't stress this one enough, especially if you have health conditions that will prevent you from qualifying for a Medigap plan later.

The second is to use a GI Period when losing other creditable coverage to apply for certain Medigap plans without health questions.

The last is to apply for a Medigap plan and answer health questions.

Perhaps you have missed your Medigap OEP and are not in a GI situation. Or more common, your current Medigap plan has had a couple of rate increases over the years, and now you'd like to switch carriers to try to reduce your premiums.

To qualify, you will need to answer a page full of medical questions before submitting your application to a Medigap carrier. That carrier will assign an underwriter who will review your application and your medical records and decide whether to accept you for coverage or issue a decline.

What Should You Expect from Medigap Underwriting?

Each insurance company has its own application for Medigap. That application will usually include at least one page of health questions. So whenever you are outside of your one-time Medicare OEP, you can expect questions about whether you have ever been diagnosed with certain conditions. You may believe that you don't have a health condition. However, if your medical record shows that your doctor diagnosed you differently, that will matter to the underwriter.

Some health questions will ask about a recent period. It's common to see questions about the last two to five years of your health history. For some of these questions, if a health event occurred several years ago and is no longer relevant, the carrier may not see it as a problem.

Most applications will have a section where you must be able to truthfully answer no to all of the health questions in that section, as indicated on the application. Answering yes to one of these questions will result in an automatic decline with most carriers. When an agent is taking an application by phone from a potential new client, if the client answers yes to one of these questions, the insurance company shuts down the application. The insurance company won't even allow us to submit it. When that happens, you are not eligible for that coverage.

Here's an example of one of those yes-or-no questions that might cause a specific company to decline coverage.

"In the past three years, have you been diagnosed with, received any treatment, or been prescribed any medications for the following conditions:"

- Internal Cancer
- Congestive Heart Failure
- Stroke or Transient Ischemic Attack
- Conditions that Required a Stent
- Chronic Obstructive Pulmonary Disease or Emphysema
- Osteoporosis with Fractures
- Rheumatoid or Disabling Arthritis
- Parkinson's Disease
- Multiple Sclerosis
- Lupus
- Alzheimer's/Dementia

Notice here that the carrier is asking about serious major health events or chronic, incurable health conditions. These often cause an automatic decline. If there is a carrier that will accept you, it might cause them to "rate you up." They come back to you offering the policy but at a significantly higher monthly premium.

It's common for carriers to decline an application when there has been an inpatient hospital stay in the last 90 days or when you've just left a skilled-nursing facility.

The good news is that many applications do get approved.

So now you know a little bit about the kinds of Medigap underwriting questions you will face. Let's talk about how various health conditions or procedures could affect you.

Minor Health Conditions—Likely Approval

The health questions on a Medigap application usually don't concern minor things like seasonal allergies or the flu. Likewise, they don't care if you had two colds last year or a urinary tract infection that quickly cleared up with a round of antibiotics. Certain injuries are a nonissue as well if you are fully healed and done with treatment.

You might take maintenance medications for high blood pressure or cholesterol. Minor health conditions for which you take maintenance meds are often not an issue unless they occur alongside another more serious condition. Likewise, minor arthritis is not a problem. However, they might decline coverage if you have a more severe and debilitating form of rheumatoid arthritis.

Restrictions on Body Mass Index (BMI) are usually more relaxed on Medigap plans than on other types of insurance like life insurance. Carrying a few extra pounds is not a problem, but they could decline you for morbid obesity. Every carrier will have underwriting guidelines about this. Your agent can check your height and weight against the company's guidelines to make sure you are within their acceptance range before you apply.

Pending Surgeries and Treatment—Finish Them First

If you have pending care, it's best to complete it before applying to change your Medigap plan. When it comes to potentially declinable situations, expensive pending procedures top the list. No insurance carrier wants to issue coverage to you just before you undergo a costly diagnostic test or major surgery. Most Medigap plans cover your Part B coinsurance, which is 20% of outpatient medical care costs, so they want you to get that done before applying for coverage. This is the case even if your pending surgery is for something minor. You will need to complete the operation and any follow-up visits or therapy before a new carrier will consider you.

Here's an example of how they ask this question:

"Within the past 12 months, have you been advised by a medical professional to have treatment, further evaluation, diagnostic testing, or any surgery that has not been performed?"

If you answer yes, the chances are that they will decline you.

Some carriers may also ask for a window of time clear *after* major surgery, such as knee replacements. Since "hardware" problems can occur, they might want you to wait a year or two before submitting your application.

Requirements vary, though. Ask your agent about which carrier's questions offer you the best chance of approval. At our agency, we go over this upfront so that our team can sort through which carriers will most likely approve your application. One carrier might cover certain conditions while others don't. Over time, our team has become familiar with which companies have the flexibility for specific health conditions. The carriers sometimes update their questions, allowing new possibilities, so we stay on top of those changes to know when it might benefit certain clients.

Recent Major Care—You'll Need to Wait

Medigap carriers also ask questions about recent major care. If you are receiving home health care or have been hospitalized two or more times in the last two years, it is common for the carrier to decline you right there on the application.

Likewise, if you live in a nursing home, it is not likely that any carrier will approve your application. Since people rarely go from an assisted-living center or nursing home back to living independently on their own, you should stick with your current coverage.

Here's an example of the wording on a question about major care:

"Are you currently hospitalized, confined to a bed, in a nursing facility or assisted-living facility, receiving home health care or physical therapy?"

FAQ: Will a Medigap company turn down my application for a history of cancer?

Answer: When it comes to major illnesses such as cancer, the carriers usually want you to be at least two years cancer-free and in remission. If you have had recent surgery or are still undergoing treatment, you'll likely need to wait a few years before applying.

There is currently at least one major company that will sometimes consider people with cancer or other serious conditions. However, they will likely charge you a significantly higher rate for the coverage. Suppose you are already on a Medigap plan and are applying to change plans to save on rates. You might find that it is cheaper to stay with your current carrier than to switch to a carrier that "rates you up" for a major health condition.

Chronic Health Conditions—Keep Your Current Coverage

Some illnesses are treatable but incurable. If you have a serious illness that will require treatment forever, you'll find that the questions on most Medigap applications will exclude you. Common examples include dementia, chronic lung disorders, immune disorders such as RA, MS, Lupus, HIV/AIDS, and nervous system disorders such as Parkinson's. Osteoporosis with fractures will also be problematic. The insurance company knows these conditions will require expensive lifetime care.

Major heart disorders might also prevent you from changing carriers. Arterial and vascular diseases, a history of heart attack or strokes, the use of stents or pacemakers, and congestive heart failure are some examples that will often cause carriers to decline your application. Many carriers will also decline to cover individuals with rhythm defects or valve problems.

Borderline Health Conditions—Could Go Either Way

Some conditions are what we call "borderline." Depending on the carrier and how they phrase the related question on their application, you might pass the Medigap underwriting.

Diabetes is an example of a borderline condition. If you take only oral diabetes medications or you take less than 50 units of insulin, the underwriter may approve your application. With diabetes, carriers also look at relative conditions. For example, if you have diabetes AND high blood pressure with high cholesterol or neuropathy, it is harder to get approved than if you have diabetes without any related conditions.

Here's an example of the diabetes question from one Medigap company's application:

"Do you have diabetes with hypertension requiring three or more hypertension medications to control it or diabetes requiring more than 50 units of insulin daily to control it?"

Diabetes is one condition where you need to speak with a broker who works with multiple Medigap companies because individual underwriting guidelines on this vary quite a bit. Brokers will know where you'll have the best chance to be accepted.

Another example where the area is kind of gray: mental health conditions. Generally, seeing a therapist or taking a mild antidepressant may not be an issue. However, more chronic mental disorders, such as schizophrenia, can cause declines.

Here's a question about mental health as it appears on the application for a carrier we work with:

"Do you have now or in the last two years have you been treated for (including surgery) or advised by a medical professional to have treatment for major depression, bipolar disorder, schizophrenia, or a paranoid disorder?"

Answering yes will cause the carrier to decline your application, so have a conversation with your broker if something like this pertains to you.

Auto-Decline Medications and Script Checks

Medigap carriers have access to national records regarding your prescription history. On your application, you must agree to allow the carrier access to these records. When the carrier pulls the report, they will first look to see if any disqualifying prescriptions indicate a declinable condition. For example, if you take a blood thinner, the insurance company wants to know why. They'll look closely at what other medications you take that could indicate significant health problems.

Honesty is important. Try hard to remember all the meds you've taken recently. Think back over your medication history. Has a doctor ever prescribed something for you that you didn't end up taking? This might cause a problem. Let's say that your doctor once prescribed medication for lupus. However, you didn't mention lupus on your application because you are no longer taking that medication. That's a red flag to the Medigap underwriter. You may not consider yourself to be "taking that medicine" any longer, but it still exists in your record, and you can be sure they'll ask about it.

Carriers also have lists of "auto-decline medications." These are mostly medications that treat major or chronic illnesses. By taking these prescription drugs, you indicate a health condition that might be expensive for the carrier to cover.

Sometimes a particular mix of medications is problematic. Let's imagine you take diabetes meds along with high blood pressure and cholesterol meds. The insurance company could decline your application if your doctor has recently adjusted the dosages. Carriers will look at your history with those medications and see how recently and how often your dosages have changed. Frequent or recent changes can work against you.

One set of medications that can sneak up on you is pain medications. Suppose you took a short-term round of hydrocodone while recovering from surgery. The underwriter might not consider this a problem. However, if you regularly take pain medication, that could indicate an underlying and potentially costly problem in the eyes of the underwriter. Some pain meds that the insurers might deem problematic include fentanyl, morphine, oxycodone, and oxycontin.

A Word about Medical Records

Something we've noticed over the years is that people don't always know what is in their medical records. Think carefully about this. For example, if your doctor has told you that you are prediabetic, ask him or her what he has written in your file. Did your doctor sugarcoat that health condition in conversation with you while diagnosing you in the written record? Is it an ongoing issue that you revisit each time you go in for a checkup? Perhaps your doctor told you that you were prediabetic, but what matters is what he or she wrote in your file. If your chart says "diabetes," that is what the carrier will include in its assessment. If you are unsure, ask your doctor before you apply for a Medigap plan. If a doctor prescribes a medication that you have no intention of filling, tell him or her that at the appointment and ask him or her not to prescribe it. Once your doctor prescribes it, it's in your medical record.

Submitting a Medigap Application

Once we have identified a suitable insurance company for you, we take that application from you over the phone or by e-mailing you a printable version.

Switching Medigap plans can take time, so I recommend applying for a future effective date that is two to three weeks out. Applying early gives the new insurance company plenty of time to complete underwriting and give you an answer before you need the coverage to take effect.

An underwriter may call you with follow-up questions. The phone interview is an integral part of a carrier's decision process. Underwriters will usually have questions related to your medical records and prescriptions you've taken. Occasionally, they may ask you to provide additional medical records if your doctor's office is unwilling to forward them, but this is relatively rare.

Don't volunteer any more information than what the underwriter asks you. Often, we see people get declined for information that they voluntarily offered that was not an answer to a question asked by the underwriter. Use yes-and-no answers whenever possible, but always be honest.

Even good changes in your health and medication history can be frowned upon by underwriters. Why? Because it indicates inconsistency. For example, we had a client who proudly mentioned to the underwriter that she had recently lost a hundred pounds. The underwriter promptly denied her application. A recent loss of that much weight is an example of an inconsistency in your health record. The underwriter will likely be concerned that there could be future health conditions that result from you previously carrying that extra weight around that have yet to come to light.

Bottom line: You could get declined because you shared a comment that the underwriter didn't ask you about. Don't volunteer anything other than truthful answers to the exact questions asked.

Don't Cancel Your Current Coverage Yet

It's important not to cancel any current coverage until your agent notifies you that your application is approved. Here at Boomer Benefits, we watch the pending applications daily and inform our clients immediately.

Once you receive that call, you will always need to contact your old carrier to cancel that coverage. Your insurance agent usually can't cancel prior coverage for you. Most Medigap companies want to hear directly from you if you are canceling coverage. *Never, ever assume that your agent is canceling your old coverage for you.*

Over the years, many people have contacted us for help because they had mistakenly enrolled in MORE than one Medigap plan from different agents. It is baffling when we see this. There is NEVER any reason to have double Medigap coverage. These people likely applied for new coverage and simply forgot to cancel their other coverage. They failed to notice it because the insurance company automatically drafts their premiums each month.

BOOMER BENEFITS PRO TIP: If you believe you might have more than one policy in place, you can check this inside your MyMedicare.gov account. This account shows you all policies you have in relation to Medicare. Do not assume your insurance agent will cancel your old policy. Most insurance companies will only accept a cancellation that comes directly from you, the insured individual.

The Dreaded Denial—What Now?

> **FAQ:** If I submit an application that gets declined, is that the end of the world? Does it mean that everyone else will deny me, too?
>
> **Answer:** Not necessarily.

Our team has much success with evaluating reasons for Medigap denial and examining other carriers to see where else you might have a chance. If there are no other carriers that are likely to accept you, we'll tell you. This is another area where with working with a Medicare insurance broker can save you time and energy.

It's also important to realize that just because you can't change your coverage doesn't mean you have no other options. If you can't pass the underwriting because of health conditions, you can certainly keep your existing policy (if you have one). You could also look into the other route for your Medicare, which is Medicare Advantage plans. These plans have fewer health questions. Advantage plans, though, are very different from Medigap plans. You'll need to decide if they make a better fit for you than Medigap plans. I'll help you avoid a big pitfall right out of the gate when we discuss Advantage plans in the next chapter.

Key Takeaways

In this chapter, we discussed that there are two main routes you can go with Medicare: Original Medicare with a Medigap plan and Part D or a Medicare Advantage plan.

- Medigap plans are private policies that pay *after* Medicare. They help pay your portion of Medicare cost-sharing expenses.
- A Medigap plan allows you to seek treatment with any Medicare provider nationwide.
- Your Medigap plan will be accepted by any provider who accepts Medicare regardless of which insurance company you choose for your Medigap coverage.
- Medigap plans always pay their share when Medicare first approves your claim. This makes their coverage very predictable.
- Medigap plans do not cover Part D. If you elect to stay with Original Medicare and enroll in a Medigap plan, you will also need to enroll in a standalone Part D plan if you want coverage for outpatient medications.
- The most popular Medigap plans for newly eligible beneficiaries are Plans G and N
- There is no annual open enrollment for Medigap plans.
- You will get a 6-month Medigap OEP that begins with your Part B effective date. When you apply during this period, you do not have to answer health questions on your application.
- After that period has passed, insurance companies will require you to answer health questions on your Medigap application in most states. They can decline your application for preexisting health conditions.
- Work with a broker when applying for a Medigap plan after your 6-month Medigap OEP has passed. Your

broker can help you determine if certain health conditions may present a problem.

- During an underwriting interview, don't volunteer information. Give truthful but succinct answers, such as yes or no, whenever possible.

Canceling Part B because You Joined a Medicare Advantage Plan

The first thing you must know about Medicare Advantage plans is that they do not exempt you from paying your Part B premiums. Yes, Medicare Advantage plans are usually cheaper than Medigap plans. In some urban areas, you can even find Medicare Advantage plans that have a zero premium. *Nonetheless, you still must pay for Part B.* Before I walk you through how these plans work, let me tell you about Paul's mistake so that you can avoid making a similar one.

Medicare Mistake #7—Canceling Part B because You Joined a Medicare Advantage Plan

Paul was a Medicare beneficiary who was planning to retire and live mostly on Social Security. He had a small emergency savings account, and that was it. Otherwise, he would need to budget carefully during his golden years to make ends meet.

After carefully reading about all his Medicare options, he decided that enrolling in a Medicare Advantage plan seemed like the option that he could best afford. He had found a plan offered in his county that advertised a zero premium. Of course, a plan with a zero premium sure sounded attractive. As he was reading online, he learned that when you join a Medicare Advantage plan, it pays your medical bills instead of Original Medicare. To Paul, this *sounded like* he didn't need to pay for Medicare Part B. So, he chose the Advantage plan he liked best and then enrolled himself online at the Advantage plan's website.

The plan's "Summary of Benefits" that he downloaded clearly stated *that he must remain enrolled in Parts A and B while on the plan*. Further, the online enrollment form had several statements to sign, attesting that he had read and agreed to the terms of the plan.

But who reads that legal jargon?

Paul figured he was all squared away when he received the welcome packet from the Medicare Advantage company. So, he then signed the back of his Medicare card and mailed it back to Social Security, indicating he'd like to cancel Part B. He quickly got a disenrollment notice in the mail from his Medicare

Advantage plan. They had terminated his coverage. The reason? *He had canceled Part B and therefore was no longer eligible to remain in the Medicare Advantage plan.*

It was at this point that he went online looking for help and found the Boomer Benefits website. He called us to see if we could help him straighten this out because surely his Medicare Advantage company had made a mistake, right?

I wished that was the case. Paul had made an all-too-common mistake. He believed that enrolling in a Medicare Advantage plan meant he no longer needed to pay for Part B. This mistake would ultimately cost him time, money, and a lot of hassle to straighten out. When you cancel Part B, you can't just reenroll at any time. You must wait until the next General Enrollment Period, which can leave you with nothing but Medicare Part A for months and months.

Think about that. No outpatient coverage. No coverage for doctor visits or lab tests. No coverage for outpatient surgery or physical therapy. No coverage for chemotherapy. And depending on the timing, you may get assessed a permanent Part B late penalty.

That zero premium offered by some Medicare Advantage plans is so blindingly attractive that people can think of nothing else. Paul is just one of many thousands of people who have made this same assumption and mistake. The incorrect terminology that people often use to refer to Medicare Advantage plans can contribute to this mistake. Many people and even some doctors' offices call these plans "Medicare replacement plans." That terminology causes the kind of confusion that ultimately led Paul to make his mistake.

There is a reason that you pay for Part B even when you enroll in a Medicare Advantage program. Medicare pays the insurance company to administer your Parts A and B benefits through the Medicare Advantage plan.

Why would you want to consider getting your Medicare Parts A and B benefits through a Medicare Advantage plan? Let's find out.

Option 2: Medicare Advantage Plans (Part C)

For decades, beneficiaries had only one way to cover the gaps in Medicare coverage, through a Medigap plan. If you didn't have retiree coverage through a former employer, you simply had the choice of enrolling in a Medigap plan or not. Now, however, Medicare Advantage plans are an alternative way to receive your Medicare benefits.

These plans are optional and provide you with a choice for how you get your Medicare coverage: You can get your benefits through Original Medicare or through a private insurance company's Medicare Advantage plan. Although most seniors have remained enrolled in Original Medicare, a study by the Commonwealth Fund found that the number of people enrolling in Medicare Advantage plans has tripled since 2003. About one-third[1] of all Medicare beneficiaries now get their coverage through a Medicare Advantage plan.

While the Medicare Advantage program is *technically* a part of Medicare, *the federal government does not sell Medicare Advantage plans.* The government sets rules and guidelines for the program, but private insurance companies sell and administer the Advantage plans.

There's a good reason for this, too. The federal government wisely understands that insurance companies may be more capable of reducing administrative costs for such plans than Uncle Sam. These insurance companies control costs by utilizing networks of providers, as you'll soon see.

Medicare Advantage plans do NOT work similarly to Medigap plans. Whereas Medigap plans pay *after* Medicare, Advantage plans pay *instead of* Original Medicare. Providers bill the Medicare Advantage plan, not Medicare, for services rendered.

For this reason, you can't have both a Medicare Advantage plan and a Medigap plan at the same time. It is illegal for an insurance agent to knowingly sell you a Medigap plan if you are enrolled in a Medicare Advantage plan and intend to stay on it. A Medigap plan only supplements Original Medicare. It never supplements Medicare Advantage.

The following sections describe some standard features of most Medicare Advantage plans.

Networks of Providers

Most Medicare Advantage plans utilize networks of providers. These networks may span only one or two counties on some plans. In other cases, the network might span several counties. Some regional plans even have statewide networks. Insurance companies have created these regional plans so that beneficiaries in most rural areas can have access to at least one or two Medicare Advantage plan options.

Referrals May Be Necessary

Some Medicare Advantage plans will require you to choose

a primary care provider (PCP) who must coordinate your care. You may need a referral from this PCP before you can see a specialist. The insurance companies may also require pre-authorizations for some services. We'll discuss the network types in more detail below.

Lower Premiums and Pay for Services as You Go

In general, most Medicare Advantage plans have lower premiums than Medigap plans. Some plans even have what is called a zero premium. When you have a zero-premium Medicare Advantage plan, you don't pay anything for the plan beyond what you pay for Original Medicare.

However, regardless of the plan's monthly premium, you'll also pay copays and coinsurance for medical services as you go along. Your back-end spending will depend on how often you use the plan for your medical needs. In years where you have fewer requirements for health-care services, you may spend little. In years where you have more needs for services, you may spend more.

You'll have an opportunity to review the plan's "Summary of Benefits" before enrolling in the plan to see what you can expect to pay for various services. Medicare has also set up a "star rating system" for Advantage plans so that beneficiaries can compare the quality ratings of the different plans offered in their area.

Built-In Drug Coverage

Approximately 90% of Medicare Advantage plans[2] also include a built-in Part D drug plan, per a 2020 Kaiser Family

Foundation report. Each built-in Part D plan has a set *drug formulary*, a list of prescription drugs covered by the plan.

This can work out well in some cases and not so well in others. It's great if the plan's drug formulary already includes your specific medicines. It's not so great if you like the plan itself, but then find that it does not include one or more of your medications. In that scenario, you can enroll in the plan and file an exception asking the plan to cover the medication for you. However, there is no guarantee that the plan will agree to it, so there is a chance you'll have no coverage for that drug once you are enrolled. It's better to choose a plan that already covers the medications you need.

The Part D portion of these plans will also have the same four phases of coverage that standalone drug plans have, including a deductible and the coverage gap. Check to see what the Part D deductible is on any Medicare Advantage plan that you enroll in so that it doesn't surprise you the first time you fill a prescription at the pharmacy.

Easy to Qualify

Medicare Advantage plans have no health questions. Since they have no health questions, Medicare Advantage plans are a coverage option for people who missed their six-month Medigap OEP and now cannot qualify because of health conditions.

You'll need to enroll in a Medicare Advantage plan during a valid election period, such as your IEP or the Annual Election Period (AEP), sometimes referred to as the Fall Open Enrollment Period. This is the period during which Medicare beneficiaries join, leave, or change a Medicare Advantage or Part D drug plan.

Medicare Advantage plans are also guaranteed renewable as long as you continue paying your premiums. You must continue to live in the plan's service area. *Plans cannot drop you for developing a new health condition.* If for any reason, the plan stops operating in your county, Medicare will give you a Special Enrollment Period to choose another plan.

Ancillary Benefits

Medicare Advantage plans can offer extra benefits like routine dental, vision, and hearing benefits. They may also include a gym membership. They can even provide some home-care-related benefits if they want to, like transportation to and from medical appointments, bathroom safety bars, and meal delivery.

Most of these ancillary benefits are relatively limited in nature. However, they are still "extras" that you don't get with Original Medicare. These extras appeal to many Medicare beneficiaries. Just remember that you should buy health insurance for reliable, solid coverage for serious health events or illnesses. I don't recommend choosing your health plan based solely on a dental benefit or a gym membership.

Medicare Advantage Requirements

There are two requirements to join any Medicare Advantage plan. You must:

1. Be enrolled in both Medicare Parts A & B

2. Live in the plan's service area

When you join a Medicare Advantage plan, you are not getting out of paying your Part B premium (of at least $148.50/month). Unless you qualify for Medicaid to help you pay for your Medicare Part B premiums, you will continue paying for Part B.

I'm repeating this on purpose because I have seen many people fail to understand this, which can result in a major Medicare mistake as it did for Paul.

How Do Medicare Advantage Plans Make Money?

When you enroll in a Medicare Advantage plan, Medicare pays the Advantage plan a monthly reimbursement rate called a capitation fee.

Medicare doesn't pay them chump change, either. Medicare Advantage insurance companies may receive around $10,000 or more per year from Medicare for every beneficiary enrolled in their plan. If plans achieve high-quality ratings, they can also qualify for bonuses. These bonuses make Advantage plans quite lucrative for insurance companies.

Have you wondered why you get so many solicitations in the mail for these plans? Well, this explains why. If they can attract you to enroll in their plan, they get paid. Then it's up to them to do a great job at managing your health-care expenses so that they can turn a profit.

Last—and I'm simplifying this process greatly to keep things easy—Medicare Advantage plans can also charge you a premium for the plan itself. The same 2020 Kaiser Family Foundation report that I referenced earlier found the average premiums for enrollees of Medicare Advantage plans were around $25 per month. However, in most urban areas, you can usually find a few Medicare Advantage plan options with those zero premiums we discussed earlier. Most beneficiaries, especially those in urban areas, will have dozens of plans to choose from, with their own unique premiums, deductibles, copays, cost-sharing expenses, and provider networks.

In 2021, the Kaiser Family Foundation also reported[3] that there are 3,550 Medicare Advantage plans across the nation. Thirteen new insurers joined the Medicare Advantage market for the first time this same year. The average beneficiary can choose from among 33 different plans. So many plans may make you feel hopelessly overwhelmed; how will you ever choose? Take heart, however. I'm going to show you some of the best ways to narrow down your options and find the most suitable coverage for your needs and budget.

Okay, so now you know that Congress designed the Medicare Advantage program to give Medicare beneficiaries an alternative way to get their benefits. Private insurance companies can offer beneficiaries low premiums for these plans because they are good at managing costs in various ways:

- Beneficiaries get care from the plan's network of providers. These providers deliver medical services to members at negotiated rates.
- The insurance companies can also require preauthorization for a variety of medical services to ensure that they are medically necessary or relevant. This preauthorization requirements seem to be more common with

Medicare Advantage plans than they are with Original Medicare + Medigap.

- Beneficiaries pay copays as they use medical benefits within the plan, which ultimately reduces what the plan must pay its providers.

Let's look at how the networks work and what features you can expect to find in these plans.

Medicare Advantage Plan Networks

Medicare Advantage plans are *managed care plans*. They have similar networks to the group health insurance plans that you have likely experienced during your working years.

Medicare Advantage networks will almost always give you access to fewer providers than you would have through Original Medicare and a Medigap plan because the networks are not nationwide. If you don't travel much and intend to get your medical care in your home county, this may not concern you. You can find Medicare Advantage plans with strong local networks that offer hundreds or even thousands of providers in your area.

Common Network Types: HMO and PPO

When reviewing options for Medicare Advantage plans in your area, you will quickly notice that most of the plans have either an HMO or PPO network. You are probably familiar with these from the employer insurance coverage you have had in the past but let me fill you in on the general differences.

MEDICARE ADVANTAGE NETWORK TYPES

	HMO	LOCAL PPO	REGIONAL PPO	PFFS
Network Size	One or more counties	One or more counties	Larger network area, such as statewide	Varies
Plan Availability	Most common type of MA plan	Most common type of PPO plan	Least common type of PPO plan	Only available in areas with less than 2 MA plans
Do you have to specify your PCP?	Yes	Usually, no	Usually, no	Usually, no
Are referrals required?	Usually, yes	No	No	No
Is there a maximum out-of-pocket?	Yes, in-network only (no out-of-network benefits)	Yes, in-network and out-of-network	Yes, in-network and out-of-network	Yes, in-network and out-of-network

Figure 7-1. Medicare Advantage Network Differences.

Medicare HMO Plans

HMO plans are the most prevalent. These typically have *closed-provider networks*, which means they will usually only cover services delivered by providers in the network. That network is generally local to your home county and perhaps a few surrounding counties. Some regional plans may span a larger area. Many HMO plans require that you get all your care from those network providers except in emergencies.

However, there are some HMO plans with *Point-of-Service (HMO-POS)* options that offer a bit more flexibility. An HMO-POS plan allows members to see healthcare providers outside of the network under limited circumstances for some services. You'll want to review the plan's "Evidence of Coverage" documents to understand what those situations are. You will usually pay additional costs for using the Point-of-Service option.

Plans with HMO networks also likely require you to choose a *primary care provider* (PCP) who coordinates your medical care. This provider will deliver your preventive care and become familiar with your health status. If you need to see a specialist, your PCP can refer you to a suitable specialist who is in the network.

Because HMO plans are the most restrictive, they typically also have the lowest premiums. In 2020, the average monthly premium[4] for beneficiaries enrolled in a Medicare HMO (with drug coverage) was $20/month. However, if you live in an urban area, you may find plan options with zero premiums. As we discussed, the plan has much to gain by offering you a zero premium. It makes the plan attractive to you, the buyer, and it's okay for the plan, too, because they get paid by Medicare to take on your risk. Despite the network restrictions, Medicare HMO plans are the most popular type of Advantage plan. According to the Kaiser Family Foundation, nearly 62%[5] of all Medicare Advantage members are enrolled in a Medicare HMO plan.

Medicare PPO Plans

Beneficiaries who want more network flexibility can consider a Medicare PPO plan. PPO plans usually won't require you to choose a PCP or get referrals, but this varies. Some plans may still require you to choose one. Fortunately, it's relatively easy to change your PCP selection with most plans.

Members who choose a PPO plan can see any provider willing to bill the plan, even if the provider is outside the network. Be warned, though; you'll pay more out-of-pocket for treatment outside the network. Still, people who travel frequently may find that a PPO plan fits them better.

Insurance companies can develop either local PPO or Regional PPO networks. Local PPOs build their networks in a smaller area—these networks may span just one or two counties. Regional PPOs cover much larger geographic areas, such as a whole state, to provide beneficiaries in rural areas with greater access to Medicare Advantage plan options.

However, you should think carefully about joining a Medicare Advantage plan if you live out in the middle of nowhere. We have met people who enrolled in Medicare Advantage plans where the closest available PCP in the network was more than twenty miles away. Again, that low, low premium attracts people to the plan, and they join without looking first to see if there are doctors nearby. Advantage plans may work best for people in urban areas for this reason. If you live in a rural area, check carefully to see how many providers are in the plan's network *in your area* and which hospitals the plan includes.

Since PPO plans will generally give you more freedom than HMO plans, PPO plans often cost more. In 2020, the average monthly premium for beneficiaries enrolled in a local Medicare PPO was $32/month[6], and in a regional PPO, it was $47/month. Approximately 33% of Advantage enrollees are enrolled in local PPOs, while just 5% are enrolled in regional PPOs.

In years past, another type of Medicare Advantage plan, called a *Private Fee for Service (PFFS) plan,* was a bigger player than it is today. These plans allowed you to get medical services from any provider in the nation willing to accept the plan's payment terms and bill the plan accordingly. (Some providers will happily do that, and others may not.) However, a few years ago, Medicare changed the rules on where and when carriers can offer them, so they have become increasingly harder to find.

Before we close this section, we should also look at *Special Needs* plans, which are Medicare Advantage plans designed for certain groups.

Special Needs Plans

Medicare Special Needs Plans (SNPs) are a type of Medicare Advantage plan providing coordinated care to beneficiaries with certain chronic health conditions or situations. SNPs will generally utilize HMO networks. Like other Medicare Advantage plans, they must include all the same services as Original Medicare Parts A and B.

However, SNPs tailor their plan benefits, networks, and drug formularies to meet the needs of individuals with these specific health conditions. All SNPs include a built-in Part D drug plan. If they can medically qualify, beneficiaries can enroll in them year-round, which sets them apart from other types of Medicare Advantage plans.

Let's review two of the most common types of SNPs and how they work.

Chronic Illness Special Needs Plan (C-SNP)

People with certain chronic health conditions can join a C-SNP designed to provide support for individuals with that particular illness. For example, the SNP might give beneficiaries access to a group of providers who specialize in treating a disease like diabetes or congestive heart failure. These providers work together to coordinate your care. The plan will often assign a care coordinator or case manager to assist you with keeping healthy, managing your health condition, and following your provider's orders. He or she might also help you with accessing community resources or getting the right prescriptions promptly. The C-SNP drug formulary will usually contain a robust list of drugs related to the qualifying health condition.

For you to join a C-SNP, your doctor will have to complete a chronic condition verification form at enrollment time. Your agent will provide you with the form. Your doctor can complete this form and return it so the plan can verify your eligibility.

Chronic Illness SNPs vary by county. Insurance companies get to choose where they will offer these plan designs, so you'll have to check their availability in your area.

Dual Eligible Special Needs Plans (D-SNP)

People who qualify for both Medicare and Medicaid are eligible to enroll in a D-SNP.

The costs to join a Medicare D-SNP are usually little to nothing. You can expect to spend little on deductibles, copays, and coinsurance for Parts A and B services provided by the plan. Many plans have a zero premium because Medicaid pays any plan premium for you.

Dual Special Needs Plans often also tend to offer richer ancillary benefits beyond just dental, vision, hearing, and gym memberships. These might include:

- Quarterly benefits for over-the-counter products
- Telemedicine services
- Transportation to and from doctor appointments or trips to the pharmacy
- Meal delivery at home

Other Things to Know about Medicare Advantage Plans

There are a few other things everyone should know about Medicare Advantage plans, so I'll explain them. Knowing these points ahead of time can help ensure that you don't overlook something important.

"Summary of Benefits"

Before enrolling in any Medicare Advantage plan, you should carefully review the plan's "Summary of Benefits." You are responsible for paying deductibles, copays, and coinsurance as you use health services inside your Advantage plan. The "Summary of Benefits" will tell you precisely what you should expect to pay as you use plan services.

For example, a plan's summary may show that you pay a $10 copay at the primary care doctor, a $50 copay when seeing a specialist, and a copay of $200 per night for an inpatient hospital stay. An ambulance ride may have a copay of $200 to $300. Your plan summary will list a whole bunch of typical medical services and what those services will cost.

There are several types of services where Medicare Advantage plans tend to charge you a percentage of the service's cost. It is common for people on Medicare Advantage plans to pay up to 20% for durable medical equipment, oxygen, chemo-therapy, radiation, Part B drugs, and dialysis. Keep in mind that every plan is different, and benefits in some areas, like Florida, are richer than others. Just remember that those are some of the services that will require you to *pay a percentage instead of a flat copay.*

My point: *You'll want to know which health-care services on the plan will cost you the most money.* Fortunately, *all* Medicare Advantage plans do have a maximum out-of-pocket limit to protect you from spending beyond a specific dollar amount on Parts A and B services.

Maximum Out-of-Pocket Limit (MOOP)

When we discussed Medigap plans earlier, we talked about the fact that they have higher premiums because of comprehensive coverage on the back end. You will often have fewer cost-sharing expenses as you use medical services when enrolled in a Medigap plan.

With Medicare Advantage plans, it is different – you pay as you go. You'll often find lower premiums (than Medigap) for the plan itself, but that's because you'll pay copays for health services as you go along. Thus, Medicare requires all Advantage plans to set a maximum out-of-pocket limit on your Parts A and B expenses in any calendar year. Plans can set this limit as high as $7,550, and often they do, but it varies. You might find a plan in your county with a lower limit.

Let's look at this in the worst-case scenario. Say your plan has a $7,550 MOOP. You are diagnosed with cancer and pay 20% for your chemo treatments. When you have personally spent

$7,550 that year on Parts A and B services, the plan must cover the rest of your Part A and B cost-sharing for the remainder of the year.

This MOOP resets every year, so you could spend more than $7,550 in a short period if your illness occurs toward the end of the year, and you are still treating in the new year. In January, your spending toward your MOOP starts over.

Consider this feature carefully. Consider also that your Part D expenses will be in addition to the MOOP. Do you have enough money in your savings to weather a worst-case scenario? If not, you may find that Medigap provides more peace of mind.

We tell our clients who are considering Medicare Advantage plans to set aside a rainy-day fund. You could set aside a bucket of money that you don't touch for anything other than medical spending. Then you are prepared for higher spending in a year where you have more medical needs and use your plan more than usual.

If your plan is a PPO, it will probably have a separate in-network and out-of-network limit. We had a client a few years back who developed lymphoma. She lived in Austin but chose to seek treatment at M.D. Anderson in Houston, which was outside the plan's network. Her plan had a $6,700 in-network limit and a $10,000 in-and-out of network (combined) limit. Because she sought treatment outside the network at M.D. Anderson, she did spend $10,000 on her treatments that year. She was prepared for this, though, because our team had carefully explained how out-of-network benefits work. Fortunately, she was in a position to pay it.

When working with our clients at Boomer Benefits, we often find that Medicare beneficiaries confuse the deductible with the Maximum Out-of-Pocket Limit (MOOP). Before we move on, let's clarify that point:

A deductible is an amount that you pay upfront, out of your pocket before any benefits kick in.

A Maximum Out-of-Pocket Limit is the maximum the plan allows you to spend in one year on Parts A and B services covered by your plan. The insurance company keeps track of every dollar you spend on your deductibles, copays, and coinsurance. If your spending reaches that limit, the plan then covers 100% of your Part A and B covered services through the end of the year.

Remember, the maximum limit that Medicare allows for the MOOP is $7,550. While not all Medicare Advantage plans will set the MOOP that high, some of them will. Keep in mind that not all Medicare Advantage plans will set the MOOP that high, but some may. Take that into consideration if you plan to shop for a Medicare Advantage plan in 2021.

BOOMER BENEFITS PRO TIP: I mentioned this briefly above, but it's important. I wanted to state it again here in bold print. The MOOP (Maximum Out-of-Pocket Limit) for Advantage plans does NOT include what you spend on Part D. Your drug copays and coinsurance are in addition to that. Therefore, you will likely spend more than the MOOP if you are also taking any outpatient medications. Part D medications have their own separate out-of-pocket limit called a TROOP, which we covered earlier.

Annual Homework

I like to tell our clients that Advantage plans come with homework. Believe it or not, we have some clients who enjoy this process. Your homework is to review your coverage annually.

Unlike Medigap plans, whose benefits do not change annually, both Medicare Advantage plans and Part D drug plans change every year. Plans refile their contracts with Medicare from year to year. Your plan's benefits, formulary, pharmacy network, provider network, premium, and/or copayments and coinsurance may change on January 1 of each year.

Each September, your plan will send you an "Annual Notice of Change" packet that details all the upcoming changes. You need to sit down and carefully go over it each year and decide whether you wish to stay with the plan (which will automatically renew) or change to a different plan.

Our team takes thousands of calls each fall from our beneficiaries enrolled in Medicare Advantage plans. They want our help with evaluating if they should stick with their current plan or switch to another option in their county. They are doing exactly what they should—reviewing the changes in their plan to decide if they want to stick with their plan for the next year or change.

Physician Contracts

You would never want to enroll in a Medicare Advantage plan without first checking to see if your doctors are in the network. However, doctors can join and leave networks midyear. At the same time, Medicare Advantage plans have lock-in periods for certain parts of the calendar year.

If your doctor leaves the network midyear, you may have to find another provider in your network to treat you until the next applicable election period. For example, when the AEP comes around in October, you can use that opportunity to switch to another Advantage plan. You can also return to Original Medicare instead. However, in most cases, you will have to answer health questions to get a Medigap plan, assuming your 6-month open enrollment window for Medigap has passed.

Let's take a closer look at enrollment periods as they relate to Advantage plans.

Enrollment Periods for Medicare Advantage Plans

While it is easy to qualify medically for Medicare Advantage plans, you can typically only join or leave them during valid election periods. Your first chance to join one comes during the same 7-month IEP during which you join Medicare. After that, you can only enroll in, change, or disenroll from a Medicare Advantage plan during two other standard enrollment periods or during a Special Enrollment Period due to a defined circumstance.

The Fall Annual Election Period (AEP)

The next chance to enroll in a Medicare Advantage plan is one we have already mentioned, the *Annual Election Period*, also referred to as the *Fall Medicare Open Enrollment*. It runs from October 15 to December 7 each year. I prefer to use the term *Annual Election Period* because there are too many other "open enrollment periods." This overuse of the phrase "open enrollment" makes Medicare even more confusing for so many Medicare beneficiaries like you.

During the Fall AEP, you can:

- go from one Medicare Advantage plan to another; or
- leave Original Medicare and enroll in a Medicare Advantage plan; or
- leave a Medicare Advantage plan and return to Original Medicare.

You can also enroll in, change, or disenroll from Part D drug plans during these periods, as discussed in another chapter.

The Medicare Advantage Open Enrollment Period (MAOEP)

Starting in 2019, Medicare reinstated a window that used to exist before the ACA legislation discontinued it. This window, the MAOEP, helps Medicare Advantage enrollees leave their current plan to enroll in a different one.

Every fall, thousands of beneficiaries join Medicare Advantage plans without understanding how they work. They often enroll online without knowing that the plan has a network. It's common for them to figure this out in January or February when they try to make an appointment and learn their doctor's office is not in the Advantage plan's network. Sometimes, beneficiaries forget to check the drug formulary, too. They don't realize that their plan doesn't cover one or more of their medications until they are standing at the pharmacy counter in sticker shock.

The MAOEP gives these people a chance to make things right. It runs from January 1 to March 31. It allows beneficiaries enrolled in a Medicare Advantage plan to make *one switch* to either another Medicare Advantage plan or back to Original Medicare. At this point, they can also pick up a standalone drug plan if returning to Original Medicare.

Medicare Advantage
Open Enrollment Period (MAOEP)
January 1 - March 31

Figure 7-2.

BOOMER BENEFITS PRO TIP: You cannot use this window to go from Original Medicare into a Medicare Advantage plan. It only applies to people already enrolled in a Medicare Advantage plan who wish to make a change.

Special Election Periods (SEP)

Medicare has quite a few special periods that allow beneficiaries to make a change in certain circumstances. For example, if you move from one county to another, you may lose your Medicare Advantage plan. Medicare will give you a Special Election Period (SEP) to join a new one in your new county.

You might also qualify for a SEP if you lose access to Medicaid, which causes you to lose eligibility for your D-SNP Advantage plan. There are quite a few unique situations that can qualify you for a SEP. Medicare can grant these SEPs to you when they do occur. One that I want to cover is the SEP Trial Right period.

The Trial Right Period

Suppose you choose to join a Medicare Advantage plan right out of the gate at age 65 during your IEP for Medicare. You'll have 12 months to change your mind. You can use the Trial Right SEP anytime during those 12 months to return to Original Medicare and a Part D drug plan. You can also enroll in a Medigap plan with no underwriting.

Let me share an interesting story on how this window came in handy for one of our clients years ago. Larry was a close friend of a group health insurance broker who had an office in the same building as Boomer Benefits. From the start of my call with Larry, it was clear that he wanted a Medicare Advantage plan because of the price. He listened politely to all his options, but he loved the idea of a zero premium Advantage plan.

Here in Dallas-Fort Worth, numerous big brand-name insurance companies offer zero-premium plans. Larry shared that he considered himself a great candidate for Medicare Advantage because he was in good health and didn't take many medications. In his view, paying more for a Medigap plan didn't make sense when he didn't go to the doctor all that often. We were able to find a few Medicare Advantage plans that his primary care doctor accepted. Larry chose one that operates a large network in the Dallas-Fort Worth area.

About ten months into his first year on the plan, Larry began having health issues. His stomach became extended, and when he went to the emergency room, the doctors found that he had fluid in his abdomen. They soon found that his liver was failing, even though he didn't have hepatitis or other factors that would have made him high-risk.

Because Larry was in a Medicare Advantage HMO plan, he had to return to his primary care doctor to get a referral to see a hepatologist. When the approval came through, Larry found that the first available appointment to see this specialist was in eight weeks. His primary care doctor tried to find him another hepatologist. However, he faced the same long wait for an appointment at the other specialist's office. Meanwhile, Larry was regularly returning to the emergency room to have fluid drained from his stomach cavity.

Larry called into our Client Service Team for the free help that this team offers our clients for situations like this one. Our team set to work tracking down all the hepatologists in the entire network, which included more than five counties in and around Dallas-Fort Worth. It wasn't that hard because there were only six hepatologists in the network.

One of my team members managed to snag an appointment for Larry that was only two weeks out. However, the provider's office was in far North Dallas, which was almost an hour's commute from Fort Worth for him while he was very sick. At this point, we recommended that he use his one-time SEP Trial Right to leave the Medicare Advantage plan (in the tenth month of his plan) to return to Original Medicare. This SEP also enabled him to enroll in a standalone Part D drug plan and get a guaranteed issue right to purchase a Medigap plan without health questions.

He immediately agreed. Inside of a week, we had canceled

his Medicare Advantage plan and found him a Medigap plan and drug plan. We located a hepatologist on Original Medicare that could see him much sooner.

We've since used the SEP Trial Right to help other beneficiaries out of similar circumstances. People who leave a Medigap plan to enroll in a Medicare Advantage plan for the first time can also use the SEP Trial Right to leave the plan in the first 12 months and return to Original Medicare. They will have a GI window to re-enroll in their previous Medigap plan with no underwriting. You can only use this SEP once in your lifetime.

I share Larry's story not to discourage you from a Medicare Advantage plan but rather to demonstrate the value of the SEP Trial Right election period. We have many clients happily enrolled in Medicare Advantage plans. If you like, you can join our Medicare Q&A with Boomer Benefits private Facebook group and ask them what they like about their plans.

There is a good reason why these clients are happy with their plans: We do a thorough job of sharing all the pros and cons with our clients *so that there are no surprises* later. We don't gloss over or sugarcoat anything. Most of our clients take our advice on setting up the rainy-day fund if they decide to enroll in a Medicare Advantage plan.

Our Client Service Team manager also asked me to share something with you about the Trial Right, since her team helps people use this SEP every year.

Don't wait until the last minute when using this one-time SEP. You need to apply for the Medigap coverage early enough to get it into place while still giving yourself enough time to disenroll from the Medicare Advantage plan once the Medigap company approves your application. You'll also need time to search for and enroll in the right drug plan. You can't do that until you have disenrolled from the Advantage plan.

> **BOOMER BENEFITS PRO TIP:** Remember that these enrollments are ALL regulated by federal government systems. They take time. Don't wait until month 11 to start looking into your options to exercise your SEP Trial Right.

Other Medicare Plans

There are a couple of other types of Medicare health plans that I want to briefly mention here because you can still find them in a handful of states.

Medicare Cost Plans

While Medicare Cost plans are not technically Medicare Advantage plans, enrollees have similar access to a network of physicians and hospitals. Cost plans sometimes provide ancillary benefits beyond what is offered by Original Medicare, too.

However, if you wish to see a provider who isn't in the network, that provider can bill Original Medicare. You would just pay your standard Parts A and B deductibles and coinsurance. If you don't like the plan, you can leave anytime to return to Original Medicare.

Medicare Cost Plans used to operate in many areas, but today they are harder to find. There was a provision in the Medicare Modernization Act that banned Medicare Cost Plans from operating in areas where they face substantial competition from Medicare Advantage plans. The clause was not fully implemented until 2019 when it caused many Cost Plans to fold.

It's never fun to join a health plan that you like only to see it later close down and dump you back onto Original Medicare, where you'll start your plan search all over again. So consider any Medicare Cost plans in your area carefully with that in mind.

Medicare Medical Savings Account Plans (MSA)

MSA Plans are a type of Medicare Advantage plan that combines high-deductible health coverage with a savings account for medical expenses. The plan deposits money into the MSA (Medical Savings Account) each year. Members can use this money toward medical expenses until they exhaust the funds in the account. For example, the plan might have a $3,000 deductible, but it may only contribute $1,000 each year into the account. If you use all the money, you'll have an additional $2,000 to spend out of your pocket before the MSA Plan will begin paying for your medical services.

MSA plans do not include Part D coverage, so you'll want to enroll in a standalone Part D drug plan. MSA plans are also not available everywhere, so you'll need to check the "Medicare Plan Finder" tool to see if any are available near you.

How Do You Choose?

Medicare has choices for beneficiaries. By offering options, Medicare ensures that the maximum number of people can afford to pay their share of the out-of-pocket expenses that they will incur on Medicare.

As we mentioned before, sometimes having too many choices is not a good thing. In this same vein, I want to share that choosing a Medicare plan just because you have a friend who likes her plan is also not a good idea. Your choice should reflect you and your needs, health status, and budget.

There are some things—like freedom of access to any Medicare provider—that you give up when you join an Advantage plan. I want people to know that so that they can expect it and not feel surprised by it.

We sell Medicare Advantage plans at Boomer Benefits because they are popular with beneficiaries and fit nicely in some circumstances. Sometimes a Medicare Advantage plan is the only coverage someone can afford. Or perhaps they unwittingly missed their Medigap OEP and now can't qualify for a Medigap plan due to a health condition. We also see people who have done all the research and have decided that the premium savings they'll achieve with a Medicare Advantage plan is worth the risk.

I've purposely tried in this chapter to show you some of the things that can go wrong. I want you to know the facts and the worst-case scenarios. If you choose a Medicare Advantage plan, you will now go into it with knowledge on your side. It's also important to acknowledge that your health may change over time. If a year comes along where you will have to use your medical plan more than usual, can you afford the copays on the plan you are considering?

Advantage plans can come with network hassles that might frustrate you. You may have to wait for referrals as Larry did in the situation I've just described. There is a risk that you could spend quite a bit of money in a short amount of time for certain illnesses. We have had many callers over the years who loved their Advantage plan right up until they got sick. I know the risks because I've seen people live through them. In this book, I want to share them with you to help you make the most informed decision about what's right for YOU.

About 10%-20% of our incoming clients at Boomer Benefits opt for these plans, and most of them are quite happy with them. However, let me repeat that our success rate is high because we tell our incoming clients the potential drawbacks. They purchase their plan with their eyes wide open.

Make your choices carefully and understand that if you go with a Medicare Advantage plan, you may not be able to return to a Medigap plan in the future.

Key Takeaways

To recap, here are some of the most important things you'll want to remember from this chapter:

- You must enroll in Parts A and B (and remain enrolled in them) before you can join a Medicare Advantage plan.
- Joining a Medicare Advantage plan does not allow you to escape paying for Part B.
- Medicare Advantage plans are private insurance plans that pay instead of Original Medicare.
- They often have lower premiums than Medigap plans. Some plans may even have a zero premium.
- Some plans will have extra ancillary benefits, like dental, vision, or hearing benefits.

- Medicare Advantage plans have networks of providers, usually an HMO or PPO. Some plans require you to choose a PCP and get referrals to see a specialist.
- Many Advantage plans include a built-in Part D drug plan.
- You can only join or leave Medicare Advantage plans at certain times of the year.
- Medicare Advantage plans, like Part D drug plans, have benefits that can change annually. Always review the Annual Notice of Change letter that you receive from your plan in September.

As we close this chapter, it is time for me to share a GIANT mistake that Medicare beneficiaries often make when deciding which plan to choose. This mistake concerns open enrollment periods. This mistake is so ugly that it deserves its very own newspaper headline.

Let's reveal Mistake #8 in the next chapter.

Chapter

8

MEDICARE MISTAKE #8:

The Big Mistake

We offer a Medicare 101 webinar at Boomer Benefits. Thousands of beneficiaries attend to learn the Medicare basics each year. Often, I get some form of the following question, even after I cover it in detail during the presentation:

"But can't I just wait until I get sick and then sign up for a Medigap plan during the Fall Annual Election Period?"

Nope.

If I had to choose one thing about Medicare that most shocks beneficiaries, this one is it.

After all, when you hear the term "Annual Election Period" or "Open Enrollment Period," it sure sounds like you get to make any change that you want to at that time. Alas, this is not the case in most states, and many people are unaware of it until it's too late.

Medicare Mistake #8—Confusing Your One-Time Medigap Open Enrollment Period (Medigap OEP) with the Fall Annual Election Period (AEP)

Your One-Time Medigap Open Enrollment Period (Medigap OEP) lets you enroll in any Medigap plan you want with no health questions asked. The Medicare Annual Election Period (AEP) does not.

They. Are. Different.

The Fall AEP has nothing to do with Medigap plans.

You Get One Shot at the Medigap OEP

Chapter 6 covered how to qualify for a Medigap plan and explained your one-time, 6-month Medigap OEP. Everyone gets a 6-month opportunity, beginning on their Part B effective date, to sign up for Medigap with no health questions asked.

Then the opportunity is gone.

It does not recur for most people.

The primary exception to this is people who qualified for Medicare under age 65 due to a disability. They will have a second chance to join a Medigap plan without underwriting when they turn 65.

I want you to understand what I'm saying here: **You can't enroll in a cheaper Medicare Advantage plan at age 65 and then just wait until you get sick to switch to the more comprehensive Medigap coverage.**

While that would be lovely in theory, it would also cause all the Medigap insurance companies to go belly-up. So understand that if you choose to enroll in a Medicare Advantage plan, you should know that leaving that coverage later and returning to a Medigap plan a few years down the road is not a guarantee. In most states, you'll answer health questions. The Medigap carriers could turn you down for coverage.

Here is what happened to Sandy. Healthy and living on a fixed income, she liked the low premiums that a Medicare Advantage plan could provide. This strategy worked out for her for about five years until she developed rheumatoid arthritis. Her specialist prescribed Remicade, an injectable Part B drug. Since he administered this drug in his office, it fell under Part B. Her share of the costs for Part B drugs under her Medicare Advantage plan was 20%. Suddenly, Sandy was shelling out $4,500 per year on this one medication.

She contacted us during the AEP, fully expecting to leave her Medicare Advantage plan and return to a Medigap plan. She was devastated to learn that her chronic illness would likely make her ineligible for a Medigap plan. No one had ever told her that the AEP wouldn't give her a free pass into a Medigap plan.

That's why I call it the Big Mistake. Thousands of people enroll in lower-premium Medicare Advantage plans every year, assuming that they can wait until they get sick and then change to the more expensive Medigap plan.

Approval for Medigap Is not Always Guaranteed

Leaving a Medicare Advantage plan during the AEP simply moves you back to Original Medicare. As you have already learned, having only Original Medicare puts you at considerable risk for catastrophic medical spending if you develop a severe illness.

Remember, Medicare Part B has no cap on your out-of-pocket expenses. You pay 20% for eternity. For this reason, most people returning to Original Medicare want to also apply for a Medigap plan to supplement their Medicare. Unfortunately, you won't automatically qualify for a Medigap plan to go alongside your Original Medicare in most states.

A Medigap plan application includes that page of health questions we covered in Chapter 6. You must be able to answer "no" to specific questions before the underwriter will approve you for coverage (in most states). A medical underwriter will review your application. A serious illness such as rheumatoid arthritis, congestive heart failure, or COPD can disqualify you from most insurance carriers offering these plans. If you do find a carrier that will accept you, it may do so at a much higher monthly premium than the rest.

No matter your health conditions, *the order of events in changing from Medicare Advantage back to Medigap is critical:*

1. Apply for the Medigap plan first.
2. Wait to make sure you are approved.
3. THEN leave your Medicare Advantage plan.

BOOMER BENEFITS PRO TIP: When you enroll in a standalone Part D policy, the Medicare Advantage company will automatically boot you out of your Advantage plan. You need to wait to apply for the new Part D policy until after you have learned of your Medigap approval.

Jan had run into some network hassles with her Medicare Advantage HMO plan. After speaking with friends, she decided to return to Original Medicare, where she felt she would have fewer prior authorizations and no referral requirements. She first applied for a Medigap plan, and then she decided to take care of the standalone Part D plan while the underwriter reviewed her Medigap application. As soon as she enrolled in Part D, she received a disenrollment notice from her Medicare Advantage plan. She didn't know that enrolling in Part D would boot her out of her Advantage plan immediately. As a result, she endured considerable anxiety while waiting to hear if the Medigap plan had approved her. She had *not* intended to cancel her Advantage plan until she was sure of her Medigap approval.

Careful timing during a valid election period is required. For example, you could apply for the Medigap plan in October, requesting a January 1 effective date. Upon approval, you would need to enroll in the Part D drug plan and leave the Medicare Advantage plan before the AEP ends on December 7.

Sound tricky?

It is.

A Medicare insurance agent can help you avoid missteps on the order of events. We work with these plans regularly and are aware of nuances like these.

What Is the Annual Election Period For?

FAQ: If I can't use the AEP to enroll in a Medigap plan without health questions, then what is the AEP for?

Answer: The AEP is for joining, changing, or leaving your Part D drug plan or Medicare Advantage plan.

MEDIGAP OEP IS NOT THE SAME AS FALL AEP

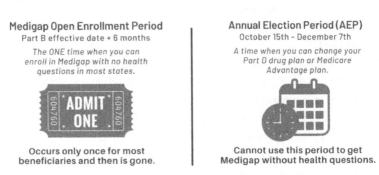

Medigap Open Enrollment Period	Annual Election Period (AEP)
Part B effective date + 6 months	October 15th – December 7th
The ONE time when you can enroll in Medigap with no health questions in most states.	*A time when you can change your Part D drug plan or Medicare Advantage plan.*
Occurs only once for most beneficiaries and then is gone.	Cannot use this period to get Medigap without health questions.

Figure 8-1.

Medicare Advantage and Part D policies require an Annual Election Period. Since both types of policies require little to no underwriting, Medicare must limit the time of year when you can join them or leave them. If they didn't, everyone would wait until they got sick to sign up for any coverage. The insurance companies providing these plans would quickly go broke. (The open enrollment period in the fall for the ACA individual health plans exists for the same reason.)

Remember also that Medicare Advantage plans and Part D drug plans change their benefits every year. Your current drug plan or Advantage plan may have changes for next year that you don't like. You will need the AEP to switch to another Advantage or drug plan if you want to.

Medigap plan benefits do not change like this; therefore, they don't need an election period. You can apply for a Medigap plan at any time of year, but most people only shop them when they have received a rate increase.

Medigap Rate Increases Are *not* Linked to the Fall AEP

Medigap plans usually DO have rate increases every year. These plans cover your Medicare deductibles, copays, and coinsurance, and Medicare itself increases those cost-sharing items each year. However, Medigap plans don't have rate increases *related to the AEP. Instead, most Medigap insurance companies will increase your rate once per year on your policy anniversary.*

If you first applied for a Medigap policy in June, your plan would usually have a rate increase each year in June. (There are a few carriers that have increases at other times or even more than once per year, so you should ask your agent about this when you enroll so you know what to expect.) Your Medigap insurance company will send you a rate increase letter notifying you of the upcoming rate change about 1-2 months before it goes up.

When our clients get rate increase letters, they call our Client Service Team to shop their rates. Let's say that a client calls in to notify us that their Plan G is taking a $15/month rate increase on the policy anniversary. We will check all the Plan G carriers in the client's home area to see if we can find another Plan G offering a lower monthly premium. If we find another company offering a better price, we help the client apply. This involves him or her answering health questions on the application in most states. (Remember, your one-time Medigap OEP is now over and gone.) The underwriter will review your application and medical records and issue a decision. If approved, then, and only then, should you cancel your first Medigap policy. **Never cancel your current Medigap plan unless you know the new Medigap company has approved your application.**

On average, I would say most of our policyholders shop their rates every 2-3 years. Sometimes, the rate increases you incur from one year to the next are too small to warrant the hassle and paperwork for changing. *Other times, you get lucky and have no increase at all, which is rare but does occasionally happen.* And of course, there are times when you can't change your policy because you have now developed a health condition that makes you unable to pass the underwriting to change. When that is the case, you'll stay with your current Medigap plan for the long run.

You could also consider switching to Medicare Advantage during a future election period. Still, you must put pen to paper and carefully calculate what you might spend if you do so. For example, if you see a specialist twice a month at $50 a pop, those visits could quickly eat up the premium savings you would gain from switching plans.

States with Exceptions

What fun would Medicare be without a bunch of exceptions to further confuse the issue?

The switching process, as I have described here, is how things work in most states. However, there are a few states that have implemented additional Medigap protections for their Medicare beneficiaries.

States with Year-Round Open Enrollment

A few states have Medigap Open Enrollment year-round, which means you can apply for a Medigap plan anytime without health questions. While this sounds great, it can also sometimes drive the overall Medigap rates up in those states.

- In **Massachusetts, New York, and Connecticut**, Medigap insurance companies offer guaranteed issue policies year-round. However, in New York and Connecticut, Medigap insurers may impose up to a six-month waiting period for treatment of preexisting conditions if the beneficiary did not have at least six months of continuous creditable coverage before they want to purchase the new policy.
- In **Vermont**, there are also a few (not all) Medigap insurance companies that will approve Medigap plans year-round.
- In **Washington**, Medigap policyholders enrolled in Plan B through N can change to any other Plan B through N plan year-round with no underwriting. So you could start with a Medigap plan B and switch to a fuller coverage plan later on whenever you like. If you enroll in Plan A, you can switch to any other Plan A.

States with Additional Limited Periods of Open Enrollment

- In **California and Oregon**, there is a "birthday rule" that gives Medigap enrollees an annual opportunity to make changes from one plan to another. During a short period surrounding your birthday, you can switch from an existing Medigap plan to another plan of *equal or lesser benefits* without underwriting. For example, someone could change from Plan G to Plan N without health questions, but going from Plan N to Plan G would require you to answer health questions. Switching Medigap plans in these two states then allows residents to stay insured at the lowest possible premiums continually.

- In **Missouri**, there is a similar provision based on your policy anniversary rather than your birthday. You can change your policy once per year during a 60-day window surrounding your policy anniversary. You can switch to any other carrier *offering the same Medigap plan* for a lower price.

- In **Maine**, you have the guaranteed right to change your policy at any time to one of equal or lesser benefits. However, this is true only IF you haven't had any gaps in coverage longer than 90 days since you first enrolled in Medigap. Furthermore, insurance companies in Maine must offer Plan A to anyone who applies during a 30-day window each year.

Please note that most of these limited open enrollment protections won't help you go from a Medicare Advantage plan to a Medigap plan without underwriting. These rules affect existing Medigap policyholders who are trying to switch to another Medigap plan. **Now that we know that you can't use the AEP to get a Medigap plan with no underwriting, let's repeat what the Medicare AEP *is* for and how you'll remember it.**

The AEP is hard to miss. Around October 1 of each year, nonstop Medicare commercials for Advantage plans will inundate your television, radio, and e-mail inbox. Your mailbox will become stuffed with mailers and postcards. Your phone will ring off the hook with telemarketers who stalk you despite Medicare's rule against soliciting. Even going to the pharmacy isn't safe. You will likely walk in to find desks set up by agents sitting there waiting to sell you anything at the first opportunity. This flurry of Medicare activity is a pretty clear reminder that *something* is going on at this time. So, most beneficiaries know they need to do *something* during the Medicare AEP each year, but they are not sure what.

We once had a client whose son was a doctor and had told her to enroll in a Medigap plan and avoid Medicare Advantage plans because his clinic didn't like them. A few years later, she went to the pharmacy to pick up a prescription during the AEP. While there, an agent at a booth convinced her to enroll in a Medicare Advantage HMO plan with a zero premium. She was very proud to have lowered her premiums so much. That is, until she told her son. He reminded her that he had told her to stick with Original Medicare and a Medigap plan for her supplemental coverage. She called us in tears, needing our help to switch back. Fortunately, our Client Service Team went to work fixing her mistake using her SEP Trial Right.

The point is this: It is easy to fall victim to the salespeople bombarding you from every angle. Don't enroll in any plan on a whim or at a moment's notice. Always do the careful research that I have outlined for you in this book.

Having read this book, you are already a step ahead of the rest. *You know that this fall period is only for changing your Medicare Advantage plan or your Part D drug plan.*

What Does *not* Change During the AEP?

You do not need to fiddle with your Medigap plan AT ALL during this period. None of your benefits on your Medigap plan are changing. Medigap plan benefits on popular plans like Plan G and Plan N do not change from year to year.

Even if you choose a less popular plan like the High-Deductible G, the deductible adjusts only slightly each year. Likewise, Medigap plans like K and L that have an out-of-pocket limit will see a *minimal increase* in that limit each year.

No core benefits are changing.

Your Medigap premium may change between October and December if you initially bought your policy during those months. But that premium change is a function of your policy anniversary, not because of the AEP.

If you have Medigap and Part D, you can concentrate on getting your Part D done during the AEP since it has a deadline. Then you can focus on shopping the rate of your Medigap plan (IF you had an increase due to a policy anniversary) afterward. Don't feel like you need to tackle both things at once. There is no deadline for changing your Medigap plan. You can apply for a new Medigap plan at any time of year. (I'll share more with you about how to review your annual plan decisions in chapter 10.)

Key Takeaways

Pat yourself on the back for getting all this knowledge under your belt. You know about eight Medicare mistakes to avoid. Here are the important points we covered in this chapter:

- *The Medigap OEP and the Fall AEP are for entirely different things.*
- The Medigap OEP is a 6-month window, starting with

your Part B effective date, during which you can enroll in a Medigap plan with no health questions asked.

- The Fall AEP, on the other hand, is a period for making changes to Part D drug plans or Medicare Advantage plans.
- **You cannot use the AEP to sign up for a Medigap plan with no health questions in most states. The AEP does not concern Medigap plans at all.**
- If you wish to leave a Medicare Advantage plan and return to Original Medicare and a Medigap plan, the order in which you make these changes matters.
- While Medigap plans do have rate increases each year, those usually occur on your policy anniversary. This means you don't have to worry about shopping your Medigap plan in the AEP. Your Medigap plan isn't changing any of its benefits from one year to the next.
- Here's a good rule of thumb on shopping your Medigap plan. Do so whenever your insurance company sends you a notice of a rate increase, which again, is usually around the time of your policy anniversary.

Knowing that the AEP only pertains to drug plans and Medicare Advantage plans will save you much unnecessary work, anxiety, and hassle in the years ahead.

It's time to decide which of the two routes is best for you. You can choose Original Medicare with a Medigap plan and standalone Part D drug plan, or you can enroll in a Medicare Advantage plan. Maybe you are already leaning toward one type of coverage or the other. Before you choose, it's important to check with your doctors and hospitals about which type of coverage they accept. I'm going to tell you exactly how to ask the right questions in the next chapter.

Part
5

MAJOR DECISIONS:

Which Insurance Plan Should You Select?

Should You Stick with It?

Chapter

9

MEDICARE MISTAKE #9:

Asking Your Doctor's Office the Wrong Questions (or not Asking at All)

When Kathy turned 65, she decided to enroll in a Medicare Advantage HMO plan that her friend Sally raved about whenever they discussed Medicare. The plan sounded good, with a low monthly premium and a gym membership to boot. Kathy went straight to the plan's website and enrolled herself in the coverage. After all, if Sally was so happy with the plan, why wouldn't Kathy feel the same?

Three months after her enrollment, Kathy made an appointment with her doctor about some shoulder pain she had been experiencing. On the day of her appointment, the office staff asked for her insurance card. When Kathy handed it over, the receptionist handed it back to her with a frown, explaining that Dr. Jacobs didn't participate in that plan.

What? Don't all doctors accept Medicare? You know by now that while most accept Original Medicare, far fewer participate in Medicare Advantage plans. Now Kathy found herself stuck in a plan with no access to her doctor. She could have avoided this situation if she had known how to ask the right questions before choosing coverage.

Doctors and Medicare

When I say that most physicians in the United States do accept Medicare, by that I mean Original Medicare. So, most of the time, when someone like yourself ages into and sticks with Original Medicare, there is no problem. That someone (and you) can continue to see the same doctors you both have seen while under 65.

However, not all doctors accept Medicare Advantage plans. If they do participate in a Medicare Advantage plan in your local area, they rarely participate in all of the available plans. Some urban areas have 20–30 different Medicare Advantage plans. Doctors would find it impossible to participate in all of them. Your doctor may also have a reason why he or she does or doesn't participate in specific Medicare Advantage plans. You'll want to know what those reasons are so that you can decide if it discourages you from participating in that plan.

It gets even trickier when you start dealing with specialists. You may find that your primary care physician (PCP) participates in one Medicare Advantage network, but your endocrinologist or orthopedic specialist does not. If you are in an HMO plan, you now face another problem: Your PCP can't set up a referral to a specialist who isn't in the plan's HMO network.

How can you avoid this problem and select the right plan? The key is in doing some careful research ahead of time, especially if you see more than one doctor. You'll start by contacting the most crucial doctors' offices to determine whether they participate in any Medicare Advantage plans. This process will help to inform you about which Medigap or Medicare Advantage plans would best suit your needs.

How Do You Ask your Doctors about Plan Participation?

The first question you need to ask each of your providers is: "Do you accept Original Medicare?"

Most of the time, the answer is yes, because as I've mentioned, around 93% of physicians accept Original Medicare.

If your doctor's office tells you yes, you'll know that ANY Medigap plan will work for you. All Medigap plans allow you to see any provider that accepts Medicare, so it doesn't matter which insurance company offers the Medigap plan. If your doctor accepts Medicare, your Medigap plan will pay just as it is supposed to.

If you are leaning toward a Medigap plan, you can also ask your doctor: "Do you accept Medicare's assigned rates?" We discussed excess charges in an earlier chapter. Medigap Plan G covers these, but Plan N does not. If your doctor says no, then you'll know that Plan G is a wise choice, since it covers excess charges whereas Plan N does not.

The next question to ask is a bit trickier. You'll need to ask:

③ **"Do you participate *in the network* for any Medicare Advantage plans?"**

Sometimes the staffer at the doctor's office doesn't know what an Advantage plan is. If you run into this, try asking if the doctor accepts any Medicare replacement plans. This term, "Medicare replacement plans," is a misnomer because nothing ever truly replaces your Original Medicare. You've already learned that you first need to enroll in both Medicare Parts A and B before joining a Medicare Advantage plan.

However, many doctors' offices think of them as replacement plans and stubbornly persist in calling them that. You can try asking your question using those words: "Do you participate in the network for any Medicare replacement plans?"

Suppose the staffer tells you yes, that the doctor does participate in one or more Medicare Advantage plans. You need to ask *which* Medicare Advantage plans.

Your Questions Must Be Specific

We see many Medicare beneficiaries go wrong here when they are trying to do all this work themselves without consulting an agent or reading a book like this one. They ask the wrong questions, which leads to problems like Kathy experienced in our earlier example.

Here is an example of the **wrong** question to ask:

"Do you take Blue Cross Blue Shield?"

I'm just using Blue Cross Blue Shield as an example here since they are a well-known brand. You can switch it out with any other insurance company name, but the result is the same: **It's not**

specific enough. The doctor's office may tell you that yes, they take Blue Cross Blue Shield. You smile and hang up the phone and proceed to enroll in the Blue Cross Blue Shield Medicare HMO you have been considering. The problem is that the staffer *may have meant* that they accept Blue Cross Blue Shield Medigap plans, not BCBS Medicare Advantage plans, which are different. Alternately, she may have meant that they take the Blue Cross Blue Shield Medicare Advantage PPO, but that doesn't mean they are also in the network for the company's Medicare HMO.

> **BOOMER BENEFITS PRO TIP:** The doctor's office employees often don't know enough to warn you about the differences among various plans! You need to be deliberate about how you ask these questions.

Here at our agency, we assist our incoming clients with this process of narrowing down their plan options. Let me give you some pointers based on our experience. When you speak with a doctor's office about which plans the doctor participates in, ask them for specifics like this:

"Do you participate in any Medicare Advantage plans?"

If they say yes, you ask: "Which plans is the doctor in the network for?"

If you are checking on one specific plan that you are particularly interested in, mention the plan by its name: "Do you participate in the network for the ABC Insurance Medicare Advantage Gold HMO?"

See how specific that is? That's how specific you need to be when you ask these questions. Use the actual plan name.

So, that's *your first step*. However, there is one more step that is even more important, and you should never enroll in any Medicare Advantage plan without doing it.

> DUE DILIGENCE: Cynthia has been seeing the same endocrinologist for her diabetes for the last ten years. Upon turning 65, she speaks with her doctor's office manager, who tells her that they accept the ABC Insurance replacement plans. Understanding that ABC Insurance may offer several Medicare Advantage plans in her area, Cynthia asks the manager for the specific name of the plan in which her doctor participates. After learning that her doctor participates in the ABC Medicare Regional PPO, she confirms with her primary care doctor that he is also in the network for this same plan before enrolling.

Check the Plan Directory

Every Medicare Advantage plan that operates a network has an online directory of all the providers that participate in its plan. The *single most critical step* that you can take is to confirm your doctor(s) participates in the network and *appears in that plan's directory of providers*.

Calling the doctor's office about plans helps you to narrow down your options. For example, you may find out the doctor doesn't participate in *any* Medicare Advantage plans. Then you know that you must choose a Medigap plan if you want to continue seeing your doctor. Or you might find out that the doctor accepts only one or two Medicare Advantage plans. Then you can look carefully at those plans to see if you like the benefits. Your doctor's office may tell you about a particular Medicare Advantage plan in which they participate. It's critical that you go to the plan's website and verify that information. Look up the specific plan and seek out its "find a doctor" feature. Search the directory to confirm that the plan shows that the doctor is in the network. While you are there, check on the hospitals in the network, too. You may have a preferred hospital. You'll need to know whether you can go to that hospital with your new coverage. If you have providers that you are not willing to change, you should not enroll in a Medicare Advantage plan until you confirm those providers appear in the plan's online directory.

Last, I should mention that some doctors will encourage you to enroll in a specific Medicare Advantage plan. We have had several clients with Medigap plans mention the "hard sell" their doctor's office gives them about a Medicare Advantage plan every time they go in for an appointment. These doctors may have various reasons for doing so. That's fine, but don't enroll in that plan to please someone else. Make sure that all the other benefits in that plan are a fit for you first. Choosing the right plan requires research and asking the right questions, so take time to decide. Putting in some time and effort on this will benefit you in the long run.

ASK YOUR DOCTOR SPECIFIC QUESTIONS

Ask your doctor's office about the specific plan you are considering, not just the insurance company.

ABC Insurance Carrier
Medicare Advantage
Gold *HMO*

What network is
Dr. Example in?

ABC Insurance Carrier
Medicare Advantage
Choice *PPO*

Figure 9-1.

A Word about Multiple Doctors

Doing this work can become especially tedious if you see several specialists. The chances of finding a Medicare Advantage plan that your PCP participates in is relatively high. However, if you see seven different doctors, finding a plan that all seven of those doctors happen to participate in is more difficult and sometimes impossible.

When we do this work for a new Medicare beneficiary with multiple providers, we often find one plan where a few of those doctors participate, but not all of them. We communicate this to our clients, who then must decide whether they are willing to change the doctors that aren't in that network. If not, then Original Medicare and a Medigap plan is likely a better route.

Sadly, you are not done with your research at this point, because there's still the matter of your drug plan. If the Medicare Advantage plan includes Part D, check the plan's drug formulary to ensure it includes all your medications. It's always a bummer when you do all that work to find a plan that your doctors participate in only to find out that the plan doesn't cover your $400/month asthma medication. Then you are back to square one. At that point, you should consider whether a Medigap plan might fit you better. A Medigap plan is more likely to enable you to see all your providers since most providers accept Original Medicare. It will also allow you to choose a standalone drug plan that offers the right coverage for you.

Hard-to-Find Specialties

We've mentioned that most doctors accept Medicare. So, while you are on Medicare, you will have access to many doctors, including those who have an MD or DO and run a family practice. You'll also find nurse practitioners, physician assistants, clinical nurse specialists, internal medicine doctors, and a few others.

However, while most doctors accept Medicare, not all of them do. Medicare reimburses physicians at a much lower rate than health plans for people under 65 do, so a small percentage of doctors decide not to see Medicare patients. You will sometimes also find that a doctor does accept Medicare but is not accepting any NEW Medicare patients. His or her practice is already full.

Don't forget as well that you may find that your doctor tells you he doesn't accept Medicare's assigned rates. He is not a participating provider. However, he can still choose to see Medicare patients at a higher rate. A nonparticipating provider can charge you up to 15% over what Medicare reimburses him. You'll owe the difference or *excess charge*. There are a few states that do not allow excess charges, but in the rest of the states, you can consider Medigap Plan G that will pay those excess charges for you.

If you otherwise find that you have a doctor who just doesn't accept Medicare at all, you have a few options. You can ask if the doctor will see you at a cash discount. Some doctors may even offer an extended payment plan. If you have money saved up in an HSA, you could certainly use that to pay your non-Medicare physician. You can also ask that doctor for a referral to another doctor who does accept Medicare. Last, you can search for a new doctor using Medicare's physician compare directory. It contains a comprehensive list of doctors and other providers across the United States who accept Medicare.

There are also certain types of doctors who are less readily available once you are on Medicare, so let's briefly discuss which specialties are harder to find.

Psychiatrists

A growing number of psychiatrists are no longer seeing patients with Medicare or any insurance in general. A study published in 2014 by *JAMA Psychiatry*[1] found that only about 55% of psychiatrists accept insurance. They prefer to set their own fees, which offers them substantially better payment. Many psychiatrists could also just prefer to spend their time practicing psychiatry rather than dealing with billing headaches that may require them to hire more office staff.

Holistic Practitioners

Naturopathic medicine is quite common these days. Medicare beneficiaries may want to consider more holistic, integrative, or functional treatment options. Unfortunately, Medicare does not cover too much in the realm of alternative or holistic medicine. Chiropractic services are one exception, where Medicare will cover only adjustments (subluxation of the spine). However, if your chiropractor does take x-rays or offers wellness massage or CBD oil, these treatments are *not* covered.

Acupuncture is another exception. Medicare just announced in January of 2020 that it would cover acupuncture, with certain limits, to help treat chronic lower back pain.

Medicare doesn't usually include licensed naturopathic

doctors in its list of providers. Instead, you'll mostly find doctors with a Medical Doctor (MD) or Doctor of Osteopathic Medicine (DO) degree. You'll also find podiatrists, optometrists, or chiropractors. It's helpful to know that Medicare does include other types of health-care professionals in its network. It may cover services offered by physician assistants, nurse practitioners, clinical nurse specialists, clinical social workers, physical therapists, occupational therapists, speech-language pathologists, and clinical psychologists.

Perhaps you are willing to pay out of pocket to see a holistic provider outside of Medicare. Keep in mind that Medicare Part D only covers drugs that are prescribed by a participating Medicare provider and that have won approval from the Food and Drug Administration. Holistic doctors often treat patients with things like homeopathy, vitamins, or supplements. You will usually pay for these yourself.

Narrowing Down Your Choices

Okay, so you've made the necessary calls to your doctors' offices and checked the Medicare Advantage plan provider directories. You now have the knowledge to begin narrowing down your choices. Based on what you've found in your research, you should now feel yourself leaning toward one path or another: either a Medigap plan or a Medicare Advantage plan.

If you've decided to go the Medigap route, your next step is to get *free help* from an independent agency like Boomer Benefits that specializes in Medicare products. When a Medicare beneficiary reaches out to us for quotes, we use our software to instantly pull quotes for the Medigap carriers who offer plans in the client's zip code. *This service costs* you *absolutely nothing* because the insurance companies pay us. The premiums you pay are the same whether you get help from an agent or go directly to an insurance company.

However, by working with an insurance agency specializing in Medicare, you'll get some information you might not otherwise find. We can see which insurance companies are offering the lowest rates for a particular plan, such as Plan G. We often find several insurance companies with similar prices. Then we can go a step further and look at each insurance company's rate increases in recent years. No crystal ball will ever tell us who will have the lowest rate increase next year. However, we can at least share that information with you for consideration. We can also look at financial ratings to help us choose a carrier.

If you've decided instead to go with a Medicare Advantage plan, your agent can run a similar list of plans operating in your area. We want to find plans that your doctors' offices confirmed they participate in, which we cross-check with the plan's online directory. If your doctors participate in two or more plans, we'll next look at which of those plans offers the most cost-effective coverage for the client's specific set of medications. We'll then go over the plan's "Summary of Benefits" and drug formulary carefully to explain what costs the client will pay.

We can also review the star ratings for each Medicare Advantage plan our client is considering. If one plan has a 3.5 star rating and another has a 4.5 star rating, we might opt for the one with the higher rating. We know the plan's members have given it higher marks for good reasons.

Last, when it comes to Medicare Advantage plans, we like to

review the network size. When helping a client choose between two plans similar in costs, drug coverage, and star ratings, we'll often look to the size of the plan's network. Sometimes, one plan has 1,000 providers in the local area while another has 5,000 or more. If all else is relatively equal, we would advise the client to choose the bigger network.

While an agent will make things easier, I'm giving you all the steps here if you'd prefer to tackle them on your own. Medicare's website can help you. Register for MyMedicare.gov where you can see star ratings and run your medication searches.

What *not* to Consider

There are a few things that you may worry about that ultimately may not matter as much as you would think.

The first of these is the insurance company's brand name. Many of the major health insurance carriers offer Medigap plans and Medicare Advantage plans. *However, if there is an insurance company you've never heard of that offers a competitive rate, don't decide against it for that reason alone.* Many stable insurance companies offer plans in the Medicare market. However, some of these insurance companies focus on the Medicare market and don't offer coverage in the group and individual health insurance markets, so you have never heard of them because you've never been on Medicare before. Some of these are fine companies with decades of experience in the Medicare market so don't dismiss them if they have competitive rates in your area.

Another thing that some people get all wrapped up in is the customer service department. Other than the star ratings, it's challenging to find information on which insurance companies have better customer service departments. Enrolling with an experienced Medicare insurance agency is your best bet. Agencies like mine are paid by the insurance companies to assist you with everything and anything related to your policy. You'll deal with our expert staff, not the insurance company's call center.

Consult the agency's website and read their client reviews. Do the reviews indicate that they respond promptly? Does the broker help with things like claims research and resolution, Medicare appeals, and drug exceptions? The service you'll receive once the policy is in place is important because there are all sorts of hiccups that can happen with Medicare insurance coverage. You want to have a broker with a dedicated service department to help you when those things arise.

You'll also want help with making your annual plan decisions, which is almost as important as making those initial choices. Not reviewing your coverage could mean you miss out on thousands of dollars in savings down the road.

Key Takeaways

You now know the kinds of questions you need to ask your doctors to determine which plans will enable you to continue your treatment with those doctors. Here are the important things to remember from this chapter:

- Ask the right questions to determine which plans will allow you to continue treatment with your favorite medical providers.
- Find out if your provider accepts Original Medicare. If yes, he or she will accept *any* Medigap plan.

- Find out if your doctor participates in Medicare Advantage plans. If so, which ones?
- Always check a Medicare Advantage plan's online provider directory to confirm a provider's participation in that plan before you enroll.

It's a relief to make your initial plan choice and complete that first enrollment. Sometimes the plan you initially enroll in is the plan that you stick with for years. However, you need to review that coverage annually to ensure that you are always in the most cost-effective coverage available. Simply settling into it and then forgetting about it is a bad idea that could cost you considerable money over the long run.

Chapter 10

MEDICARE MISTAKE #10:

Annual Decisions— Failing to Review Your Coverage

I wish I could tell you that after you've selected your initial coverage, everything is smooth sailing, and you are done looking at Medicare options.

Alas, that's not the case if you want to manage your dollars wisely. There are annual decisions that you will need to make about your Medicare plans. Let's review what these are in relation to whichever route you go, Medigap or Medicare Advantage.

Medigap Plans – No Annual Change in Core Benefits

Since Medigap plans *do not* change their core benefits annually, they are less time-intensive when it comes to reviewing your coverage. However, your monthly Medigap premium will go up over time because of rising medical costs due to inflation and several other factors.

Here's what you need to know.

Medicare's Rates Go up Each Year

In Chapter 8, we briefly went over the fact that Medigap plans usually have annual rate increases.

The Centers for Medicare and Medicaid Services directly control the rates for Medicare itself. It is typical for the premiums for Medicare to go up a bit each. We also usually see Parts A and B deductibles and coinsurance amounts go up annually to keep up with inflation.

For example, in 2020, the base Part B premium was $144.60/month. The Part B deductible was $198. The Part A hospital deductible was $1,408.

In 2021, Medicare increased the base premium for Part B to $148.50/month. The Part B deductible went up to $203 per year, and the Part A hospital deductible went up to $1,484 per benefit period.

Since Medigap plans cover these things for you, they, in turn, must have rate increases to continue paying for the things they are covering. When those rate increases occur, you'll ask your agent to check rates with other carriers. Your agent may find the same plan offered by another carrier for less.

Now and then, we meet someone who enrolled in a Medigap plan and has not shopped his or her rate for five or ten years but is healthy enough to pass underwriting and change to a different plan. In this case, we can often find the same plan with another carrier for hundreds of dollars less per year.

How Do Medigap Companies Set Prices?

Most Medigap companies base their pricing on your age, gender, zip code, tobacco usage, and eligibility for any household discounts.

Many companies also offer other discounts that can affect premiums. For example, they might give you a discount if you pay your premiums via a monthly bank draft. Or they might offer a household discount when two or more people in the same household purchase coverage from the same carrier.

The Medigap plan that you choose also affects your rate. Plan N will usually offer lower premiums than Plan G because you pay more of the out-of-pocket costs on Plan N.

We also previously covered that some insurance companies may offer Medicare SELECT plans where you must use certain providers or hospitals. They typically offer these plans at a lower rate than they will for the same plan that does not require you to use the network.

Beyond these things, Medigap companies can price their products in three ways: attained-age-rated, community-rated, and issue-age-rated. In some cases, the states have laws in place about how they must price the policies. For example, a handful of states require Medigap carriers to use a community-rated pricing strategy. Likewise, a few states require issue-age-rated or community-rated policies but don't allow attained-age-rated policies. Other states leave it up to the insurance companies to decide which rating method they will use.

We usually tell our clients not to get too caught up in how

the insurance companies rate their plans. **ALL Medigap plans will have rate increases nearly every year**, regardless of how the insurance company prices its policies.

Attained-Age Medigap Policies

An attained-age rating is by far the most common pricing method in the United States. Insurance companies using this rating method base your monthly premiums on the age that you attain each year. The rates will increase slowly over time as you age.

Don't let that scare you. Attained-age policies often have lower starting premiums than issue-age policy premiums in areas where both types of policies exist. Attained-age-rated policies also represent the biggest group of insured policyholders. This spreads the insurance risk out over many people, thereby keeping pricing on these policies competitive.

Community-Rated and Issue-Age-Rated Policies

Community-rated policies charge everyone who has a specific Medigap policy the same premium regardless of age (for people age 65 and older). Rates may vary based on other factors, though, such as zip code and tobacco usage. When premiums increase due to inflation and other factors, they generally go up by the same amount.

There are a handful of states that require insurance companies to use community rating. However, it is still the least common rating method since insurance carriers in other states tend to choose one of the other two rating methods.

Issue-age-rated policies are somewhat less common than attained-age policies, but in some states, they are prevalent.

These plans have rates based on your age at the time you purchase the policy. A person who is older when he or she first purchases a policy will pay a higher premium than a younger person.

While this idea seems alluring, it does not mean you will never have rate increases; it merely means rates won't go up because of age alone. The policies often have higher starting premiums to make up for the fact that future increases won't be based on your attained age. You'll want to compare prices with other Medigap carriers carefully.

People who buy issue-age-rated policies often don't realize that the policy is still subject to annual rate increases to keep up with inflation. Be wary of any agent who tries to mislead you into believing that buying an issue-age-rated policy means you will never have an increase in premiums. That simply isn't the case.

You'll also find that in some states, you may not have all three types of rating methods available. For example, in New York, state laws require all carriers to use community rating.

MEDIGAP PRICING METHODS

	COMMUNITY-RATED	ISSUE-AGE-RATED	ATTAINED-AGE-RATED
HOW IT'S PRICED	The same premium is charged to everyone who has that policy, regardless of age but can still go up due to inflation and other factors.	The premium is based on your entry age and will also go up due to inflation and other factors.	The premium is based on your current age and will also go up due to inflation and other factors.
EXAMPLES	Judy and Mike are different ages and genders but pay the same premium for Plan G through Carrier ABC.	Sue bought her plan at 65 and pays $120. Debbie bought the same plan at age 70 and pays $150.	Jeff bought his Plan G at age 65 for $120. His premium increased to $125 at age 66, and to $128 at age 67.

Figure 10-1.

How Do Medigap Rate Increases Work?

As we can see, a carrier's rating approach can affect how and when rate increases happen. Outside of the rating approach, several other factors make rate increases on Medigap policies inevitable. You can't change these factors but understanding them is helpful.

These factors include inflation, trends in medical costs in your area, and actual losses incurred by the insurance company for its members in the previous year. Most insurance companies have rate increases once per year on your policy anniversary. However, there are a few out there that may have more than one rate increase per year.

When these rate increases occur, they typically affect an entire block of that insurance company's business, not just one or two people. For example, we might see an insurance company announce a 5% rate increase for policyholders with Plan G in a particular state. Policyholders with a Plan N might see a different rate increase.

Medigap insurers can't just pick a rate increase number out of the sky. They must file their rates[1] and rating schedules and claims experience by policy duration for approval by the state. This includes filing their historical and proposed rates with a projected loss-ratio analysis. In other words, they have to provide supporting documentation to the insurance department on why they propose a rate increase.

How and When Should You Shop Your Medigap Plan?

Your insurance company must provide notice to you of a pending rate increase. They will usually mail you a letter to notify you of the amount of the rate increase and when it will take effect.

Now is the time to reach out to your Medicare agency and ask them to shop plans. Here at our agency, we use our rating software to look for any other insurance company offering the same plan letter for a lower premium. If we find savings that make it worthwhile for our client to switch, then we go through the health questions to make sure the applicant can answer no to the necessary health questions. If so, we help our client apply. Sometimes, the carrier announces a rate increase so low that you won't bother to switch carriers. However, after a few small annual increases in a row, you may want to shop for lower premiums.

Remember, Medigap plans change only their rates, not their benefits. The only thing you need to do each year is look out for your rate increase letter and decide whether you want to have your broker shop rates. This is simpler than what you'll need to do for Medicare Advantage plans, which we'll review next.

Medicare Advantage Plans and Part D

Medicare Advantage plans and Part D plans do not have midyear rate increases. However, these plans may raise their rates for an upcoming calendar year. That's not all they can change, either. Just about everything on your Medicare Advantage plan and Part D plan can change from year to year. Your premium might go up or down. The plan can also change your deductibles, copays, coinsurance, pharmacy network, provider network, and drug formulary.

Reviewing Your "Annual Notice of Change" (ANOC) Packet

Your Medicare Advantage or Part D company will send you your ANOC in September. It's vital that you sit down to review the changes for the upcoming year carefully. Take 30 minutes to carefully review this document. It will tell you if the premium is changing and if your copays, drug formulary, or pharmacy networks are changing. Most important, look for any medications that they are dropping or moving to a more expensive tier. Many beneficiaries neglect to do this, but it is critical. You don't want to find out in January—when it is too late to make changes—that your Part D plan no longer covers one of your expensive brand-name medications.

A Missed Opportunity to Save Money, Time, and Hassle

The Kaiser Family Foundation published a statistic showing that only about 8% of Medicare Advantage enrollees and 10% of Part D enrollees[2] without low-income subsidies voluntarily changed their plans in 2017. It's not because there are no savings out there. I believe that most people just don't want to open that tremendous doorstopper of a packet when it arrives in their mailboxes in September. It gets set aside for weeks and then months because who wants to read a bunch of confusing, dry, and dull information about their Part D or Medicare Advantage plan? Or, they miss it altogether because they opted to receive it electronically. It ends up in their spam folder where they never see it.

I know this because our phones at Boomer Benefits ring off the wall in January. Beneficiaries all over the country have just gotten their first January invoice for their drug plan. NOW they notice that price went up. They hit the internet, desperately hoping to find someone who will tell them that it isn't too late to do something about it.

Unfortunately, they've missed their chance to make a change.

At our agency, we post multiple reminders and notices about the upcoming AEP on our website and in our Facebook group and on YouTube. Even still, a few clients miss the AEP each year. Life is busy. Things get in the way. It's all too easy to let that ANOC packet sit there until it's too late. Mark your calendar every September and watch your mailbox for that letter.

> **BOOMER BENEFITS PRO TIP:** If you choose to receive your ANOC letter electronically, remember to look for that ANOC email every September. If you miss the e-mail when it arrives, you might forget to review your coverage changes for next year. Put this on your calendar. If you don't have your ANOC email or letter by September 30, call your carrier or find the ANOC online at their website.

If you are working with Boomer Benefits, please note on your calendar to call in every October to have us go over what's changing in your plan for next year. We can help you decide if it makes sense to stick with that coverage or use the AEP to switch to a different plan that better meets your needs.

How Do You Shop Your Medicare Advantage or Part D Policy?

Here are some questions you should ask when reviewing your "Annual Notice of Change":

- Does the plan still cover your necessary medications next year?

- Are there any coverage restrictions for those medications, such as quantity limits or prior authorizations?
- How much will you pay for generic and brand-name drugs?
- Has the monthly premium increased?
- Has the Part D drug deductible increased?

If you are okay with the changes, you don't have to do anything further. You can let the plan automatically renew.

However, if you don't like the upcoming changes, you can use the AEP to look for another plan. Use the Plan Finder Tool inside of your MyMedicare.gov account to run a quick search of Part D plans in your area for next year. Is any other plan offering coverage that will reduce your annual drug spending? You can use the AEP to replace your current drug plan with a new drug plan.

If your plan is a Medicare Advantage plan, here are additional questions you should ask yourself as you review your ANOC:

- Are your doctors and hospitals still in the plan's network next year? Check the online directory.
- Will you need a referral from your PCP to see a specialist?
- How much is the plan's out-of-pocket maximum (MOOP) for next year? Has it increased from this year?
- Do you have the funds available to cover that MOOP in the event of a serious illness?
- How much are the copays for health-care services that you know you will need? Can you afford those copays?
- Is there a medical deductible? Is there a drug deductible?

If changes are minor and you are happy with your plan, you don't need to do anything. Your Advantage plan will automatically renew on January 1.

Annual Election Period (AEP)
October 15 - December 7

Figure 10-2.

What Changes Can You Make During the Annual Election Period?

You have some choices here:

- Do nothing, and your plan will automatically renew in January.
- Enroll in, leave, or change your Medicare Part D drug plan.
- Switch from Original Medicare to a Medicare Advantage plan.
- Switch from a Medicare Advantage plan back to Original Medicare.
- Change from one Medicare Advantage Plan to another.

Keep in mind that Part D drug plans have no health questions. You can change to any other plan offered in your state.

Similarly, it's easy to enroll in or change your Medicare Advantage plan when there are no health questions for these plans.

What Are Some Common Reasons People Change Part D and Medicare Advantage Plans?

So what are some good reasons to change your Part D plan or Medicare Advantage plan? Here are some of the most common reasons that people change their plans during the AEP:

- **Your plan is dropping one of your medications next year.** Your ANOC letter will specifically list any changes to the plan's drug formulary for next year. The plan must disclose if it is dropping any medications. It must also tell you if a prescription is moving to a more expensive tier for next year. If you take an expensive brand-name medication now that your current plan won't cover next year, you may want to change during the AEP to another drug plan that will.

- **Your doctor has left your Medicare Advantage plan network.** Unlike Medigap plans, Medicare Advantage plans have a network of doctors. If you learn that one of your doctors is leaving the plan's network, you can use the Medicare AEP to switch to another plan in which your doctor still participates.

- **Your plan has a drastic increase in premiums.** Please note that the keyword here is "drastic." Inflation happens to medical insurance plans, just like it does to auto insurance plans. If your auto insurance goes up by $3/month next year, would you go to the hassle of changing it? Probably not. Likewise, if the only thing changing on your drug plan is a small increase in premium, you may decide it's not worth the paperwork hassle to switch. But if your drug plan goes up by $20/month, you will feel pretty motivated to check and see if any other plan is more cost-effective.

- **An overall increase in expenses**. You may find that several things in the plan are changing. You might see higher copays for medical visits and drugs as well as a higher deductible and a higher MOOP. If all of these little changes add up to a lot, use the AEP to research your options.

The critical thing here is not to make it more difficult than it is. If you are happy and nothing significant is changing, don't feel like you have to shop around just because you see Medicare commercials every 90 seconds on TV.

Key Takeaways

All plans will have rate changes occasionally. You don't have to worry that the rate is changing due to anything related to your health. Both Medigap and Medicare Advantage companies cannot drop you or change your benefits or your rates due to any new health condition you develop. There are protections for you in this regard. However, it's your responsibility to review those upcoming plan changes and initiate a plan change when needed. Remember these important things when reviewing your coverage each year:

- Medicare's premiums, deductibles, copays, and coinsurance often go up from one year to the next.
- In turn, Medigap policies that pay those cost-sharing items also have rate increases.

- Consider shopping your Medigap policy whenever a significant rate increase happens.
- Medicare Advantage and Part D drug plans *change their benefits* each year. They will notify you of those changes in September via the ANOC.
- Review the ANOC carefully to decide if you want to shop your Medicare Advantage or Part D policy.
- The Fall AEP is when you can enroll in, leave, or change your Medicare Advantage or Part D policies.
- Common reasons for changing include your doctor leaving the network or changes in the plan's drug formulary, premiums, or other expenses.

Chapter 11

A Checklist of the 10 Medicare Mistakes to Avoid

(and the 5 Major Decisions You Must Make)

What's Not a Mistake—Starting Your Research Early

You've now made it through the 10 Medicare mistakes to avoid and the five major decisions that you'll need to make when you begin your Medicare journey. Pat yourself on the back. You have digested so much information.

While there are many pitfalls to Medicare for the uninformed, you now know that YOU won't make them. Researching all things Medicare ahead of time is the best action you can take before you transition to Medicare. Beneficiaries who give themselves time to learn the ins and outs of Medicare and all its various parts and plans feel significantly less stressed when enrollment arrives.

Medicare Is GREAT Coverage

It's easy to fear the unknown. However, once you familiarize yourself with Medicare, you'll soon see that the coverage is pretty good when paired with the right supplemental coverage. It's coverage that I would love to purchase for myself if it were available to me.

If you stay on the path and avoid the mistakes we've covered in this book, you'll make good decisions about Medicare. You'll soon find that you think about Medicare very little. You can move on to thinking about the more fun things related to retirement.

I think it will be helpful if I do a quick recap of what you have learned in this book. Consider it a checklist of the big decisions and potential mistakes you might encounter. You can check them off as you bypass them during your "New to Medicare" journey.

The Major Decisions You'll Face about Medicare

If Medicare will be your primary insurance and you do not have retiree coverage, you will have some big decisions to make about when to enroll and what type of coverage would suit you best.

Decision: Determining Your Best Time to Enroll

When you should enroll for each part of Medicare depends on whether you are still working. Use the information I've provided in Chapter 3 to decide *which parts* you will enroll in and *when* you will enroll in them.

Decision: Will You Need Prescription Drug Coverage?

Decide whether to purchase Medicare Part D drug coverage. Protect yourself from late-enrollment penalties by saving your letter of creditable coverage from your last employer as we discussed in Chapter 5.

Decision: Choosing which Route You'll Go with Medicare

Unless you have retiree health coverage provided by a former employer or by the military, you'll want to protect yourself from catastrophic spending by enrolling in either a Medigap plan or a Medicare Advantage plan. These are the two main routes or paths that you can choose to get your Medicare and to limit your financial risk. Once you choose which route is right for you, use the proper enrollment periods to sign up. You don't want to miss certain rights and protections like the Medigap OEP that we covered in Chapter 6. Some of these are provided to you for only a limited time.

Decision: Which Insurance Plan Should You Select?

For most people, choosing coverage begins with some questions to determine which plans your doctors accept. Using the list of questions that I provided in Chapter 9 will help you to narrow the number of choices in front of you. Then you will decide which insurance company to choose for your Medigap or Medicare Advantage plan. Remember that if you choose a Medigap plan, any provider that accepts Medicare will accept your Medigap plan, regardless of which insurance company provides it. If you choose a Medicare Advantage plan, check the online provider directory to make sure your favorite doctors and hospitals are in the plan's network.

Decision: Should You Stick with your Coverage or Change It?

Once you have enrolled, your work is not permanently over. There are some annual plan decisions you must make each year if you want to ensure that you are always in the most cost-effective coverage for yourself. Re-read Chapter 10 each September for a refresher on what kinds of changes to look out for in your Annual Notice of Change letter.

10 Medicare Mistakes to Avoid

By now you should have a pretty good understanding of these mistakes and how to avoid them. Don't forget to visit our free resources to boost your knowledge on anything that still concerns you.

Mistake #1: Assuming Medicare Is Free

They say that knowledge is power, and when it comes to Medicare, that is true. If you know ahead of time that Medicare is *not* free, then you can spend extra time putting away money for your future medical costs. Familiarize yourself with the four parts of Medicare and gain a firm understanding of how each part will work for you and what they will cost you.

If you have a year or more before you become eligible for Medicare, consider opening a health savings account. Many employers offer high-deductible health plans that you can enroll in that create an opportunity for you to open this kind of account. You can contribute money to this account now. Later, you can withdraw it tax-free for medical, dental, vision, hearing, and long-term-care expenses during retirement. You can even use funds inside your HSA to pay for your Medicare premiums. However, you cannot use the funds to pay Medigap premiums.

Mistake #2: Expecting Medicare Covers 100% of Your Health-Care Costs

If you enroll in just Original Medicare, you will find yourself faced with deductibles, copays, coinsurance, and other expenses that you feel unprepared to pay. Therefore, investigate your options for Medigap plans (also called Medicare supplements) or Medicare Advantage plans to limit your financial exposure.

Mistake #3: Missing Your Initial Enrollment Period (IEP)

Everyone gets an Initial Enrollment Period for Medicare. This date is specific to you and your 65th birthday (unless you qualified early due to disability). If you are aging into Medicare, your IEP begins three months before your 65th birthday month and extends three months after your birthday.

Remember that if you are not already taking Social Security income benefits, you must initiate your enrollment into Medicare during your IEP.

You can easily apply for Medicare online with no trip down to the Social Security office required. Here's the URL to do so: https://www.ssa.gov/benefits/medicare/

Mistake #4: Skipping Part D without Other Coverage

I recommend that most of you enroll in Part D unless you have some other form of creditable drug coverage. Even if you don't take any medications, consider enrolling in the least expensive plan to have coverage if and when you need it.

You'll also avoid the Part D late-enrollment penalty.

Occasionally, we come across someone who takes no medications but is in the highest-income bracket. That high income will cause an Income-Related Monthly Adjustment Amount (IRMAA) on Part D that will make the coverage nearly $90/month even for the cheapest drug plan. If you are in this situation, I understand why you might feel reluctant to join a Part D plan. Maybe you are in a position where you can handle unexpected drug expenses should they come your way. Perhaps you'll consider delaying enrollment for a few years.

Take your time. Run the numbers. Make the best choice for you.

Mistake #5: Failing to Keep and Submit Proof of Your Creditable Coverage

When you retire from your employer and lose access to your employer health insurance, begin to keep an eye out for your creditable coverage letter. This document is precious if you have delayed enrollment into Parts B and D. File it away somewhere in a safe place with your other financial documents.

Watch your mailbox carefully after you enroll in Part D as well. Anyone who enrolls in Part D outside of their IEP will receive a Notice of a Potential Late-enrollment Penalty.

Fill in the dates of your coverage, sign the letter, and return it to the carrier in the envelope the insurance company provides.

Some insurance plans will give you an option to call in with this information instead. Consider doing both. Either way, respond so that you don't end up with a late penalty for Part D that you later must appeal.

Mistake #6: Assuming Preexisting Conditions Don't Matter

Most Medicare beneficiaries will only get one shot at joining a Medigap plan with no medical questions and no health underwriting. Your Medigap OEP begins with your Part B effective date. You have only six months from that date to enroll in a Medigap plan without health questions in most states. If you have a medical issue that may make it difficult to qualify for coverage, don't miss your Medigap OEP unless you have other creditable coverage.

Mistake #7: Canceling Part B because You Joined a Medicare Advantage Plan

The only individuals who don't pay for Medicare Part B are people with low incomes who have qualified for Medicaid or one of the Medicare Savings Programs. If you think you may be eligible for assistance in getting Part B premiums paid for you, contact your state Medicaid office for an application. Otherwise, everyone will need to pay for Part B. You must enroll in both Parts A and B before you can buy a Medigap Plan or a Medicare Advantage plan.

Even people enrolled in a zero premium Medicare Advantage plan pay for Part B.

There is only one plausible reason for canceling Part B once you have enrolled in it, and that is if you return to the workforce. If you take a job with a large employer who provides employer-sponsored health insurance, you can cancel Part B without harm.

BIG Mistake #8: Confusing Your Medigap Open Enrollment Window with the Medicare Fall Annual Election Period

The Annual Election Period in the fall has nothing to do with Medigap plans.

At All. Period. End of story.

You cannot use the AEP to sign up for a Medigap plan with no health questions.

You cannot use it to switch from a Medicare Advantage plan to a Medigap plan with no health questions.

You cannot use it to switch from one Medigap plan to another without health questions.

It is ONLY for changing Part D or Medicare Advantage plans.

People always want to hear that they can go with lesser coverage now and improve that coverage later only after they get sick. *This option does not exist in most states.*

If the coverage you really want is a comprehensive Medigap plan, invest in that coverage from the beginning.

Mistake #9: Asking Your Doctor's Office the Wrong Questions

Your doctor's office staffers rarely understand the differences between Medicare plans. The responsibility falls on you to determine whether they accept the plan. If the doctor's office accepts Original Medicare, you can sign up for any Medigap plan and know that you are covered. If your doctor's office participates in any Medicare Advantage plans, you need to get the exact plan name(s) for the plan(s) in which they participate. Double-check that information using the Medicare Advantage plan's online directory.

Mistake #10: Failing to Review Your Coverage each Year

Both Medicare Advantage plans and Part D drug plans change their benefits every year. Watch for your "Annual Notice of Change" from your insurance carrier in September. Open the packet and review it carefully. What's changing? Your monthly premiums? Your copays? One of your medications?

If the changes are minor, you can keep your current plan. It will automatically renew. If you find changes that you don't like, you can use your MyMedicare.gov portal to shop for a new plan during the upcoming AEP.

Next Steps

I hope this book has helped you understand Medicare better than you understood it before. You may have some time before you need to make your choices. We want to provide you with some resources to use that time wisely.

My team and I have assembled an amazing book bonus to help you continue your learning process and to assist you with various steps of the Medicare process. You'll find information on how to access this bonus in the next chapters, along with a glossary of terms.

NEXT STEPS

More Learning Resources

One of my favorite things about being a Medicare educator is seeing the relief on people's faces or in their written reviews when things finally begin to make sense. As I mentioned, one of the best ways to get to that moment where everything clicks is to learn about Medicare in more than one format.

You've tackled this book and read about the major decisions you'll need to make and 10 costly mistakes you'll want to avoid. If you'd like to continue that learning, we've got a list of great FREE resources to further your learning in a couple of other formats.

Something you will find in our videos, webinars, blog posts, and Facebook group are *things to watch out for as you begin using your benefits.* Our blog and YouTube channel especially offer a series of continuing education posts and videos that go over common problems that new beneficiaries run into with Medicare and how to solve them.

For example, we offer videos on how to avoid surprise Medicare bills and a series on the "Top 5 Things We Wish Every Medicare Beneficiary Knew about Medicare." These include mini-lessons on things like why you shouldn't ever pay your Part B deductible directly to your doctor's office at the time of service. We resolve these kinds of problems and issues for our policyholders daily, so we've learned how to handle them along the way. We enjoy sharing what we've learned so that even beneficiaries out there who never got the chance to work with us can still benefit from what we've learned.

All of the resources listed below are free – they won't cost you a penny.

In addition to the resources we offer at our agency, I've listed contact information here for Social Security and Medicare.

Your Book Bonus

We've created a special bonus for all of our readers which you can find on our book website. Inside the bonus, you will find access to a variety of free and helpful tools we have created to help you in your Medicare decisions. All of these items will help you cement the knowledge you've gained in reading this book.

There is also:

- a Medicare toolkit complete with helpful checklists,

flowcharts, PDF guides, and links to important Medicare forms that you may need.

- a custom Medicare calendar that calculates your Medicare IEP based on your birthday. It lists all the other enrollment periods you'll need to know as well.

- top-secret, never-before-seen videos that I filmed solely for readers of this book to increase your knowledge on a few key topics.

Access your book bonus here: https://tenmedicaremistakes.com/bookbonus

Our Medicare Blog

We have hundreds of Boomer Benefits blog posts chock full of great Medicare and Social Security information. Some examples of the topics we cover here are:

- *How to Screw Up Your Medicare*
- *Why Medicare Advantage Plans Are Bad (or Are They?)*
- *Enrolling in Medicare After Working Past 65*
- *Does Medicare Cover Cataract Surgery?*
- *Medicare Advantage Pros and Cons*
- *Medigap Plan F vs Plan G vs Plan N*
- *Medicare Won't Pay for these Six Things*
- *Can I Pass Medigap Underwriting?*
- *Switching from Medicare Advantage Plan to Medigap*
- *Social Security Basics for Medicare Beneficiaries*

Visit our blog today at: https://boomerbenefits.link/blog

Our Popular *New to Medicare* Webinars

Join me on a free on-demand webinar where I teach all the basics. Our most popular webinar is *Medicare 101: How Medicare Works as your Primary Insurance*. However, I have also filmed a webinar specifically for people with employer-sponsored retiree coverage, FEHB, VA, or Tricare benefits.

You can find the On-Demand Webinars here: https://boomerbenefits.com/new-to-medicare-webinar-on-demand/

6-Day Medicare E-mail Course

Get one lesson on Medicare delivered to your e-mail inbox over the course of 6 days. By the end of the week, you'll have a better handle on how Medicare works and what steps you can take to further your learning.

This short course comes with a free copy of our "New to Medicare Checklist" and "BONUS Medicare Costs Work-sheet." You can sign up here: https://boomerbenefits.com/learn-medicare/

Learn Medicare with me on YouTube

With over a million views and dozens of great short videos, you can choose the topics you still feel uncertain about and learn more about them in just a few minutes. Some topics we've covered here are:

- *Medicare Advantage Pros and Cons*
- *Medigap Pros and Cons*
- *How Medicare Part D Works*
- *Medicare & Employer Coverage*

- *Medicare Advantage Plan vs. Medicare Supplement: How to Choose the Best Medicare Plan*
- *Medicare Deductibles—How and When Do You Pay Them?*
- *Will Medicare Cover My Procedure?*

You can find our YouTube channel at: https://www.youtube.com/c/BoomerBenefits

Medicare Q&A with Boomer Benefits (Private Facebook Group)

Maybe you've got a pretty good handle on Medicare now, but you've still got a few lingering questions that are specific to you and your situation. No worries! I'd love to answer them for you personally. Join our free private Facebook group where you can post your questions and get them answered by my team and me. I'm LIVE in the group quite often, and you can submit questions that you'd like me to answer. We take questions about both Medicare AND Social Security. You'll also interact with other Boomer Benefits clients and followers in a community of baby boomers and seniors who enjoy discussing Medicare, Social Security, and personal finance.

Join the Facebook group here: https://facebook.com/groups/boomerbenefits

Get Free Help from Our Team

Sometimes, it helps to speak to someone one-on-one who can answer your specific questions or do a slower walkthrough of any aspect of Medicare. My team stands ready to help you. We are licensed in every state except New York and Massachusetts. Give us a call at 817-249-8600 or request a phone appointment here: https://boomerbenefits.com/find-the-right-medicare-plan-for-me/

The Benefits of Working with an Independent Medicare Agency

Medicare insurance agencies like Boomer Benefits don't cost you a dime. We are paid by the insurance companies to help you sort through the myriad plan options out there and enroll in the right coverage.

We don't just help you once at your initial enrollment. We provide free claims support for the life of your policy, and that is what we are known for.

While there are many agencies out there in the world, few of them have the legendary Client Service Team that we do, which provides full support for problems and hiccups that just seem to happen with Medicare. Whether Medicare has denied your claim due to mis-coded provider bills, or you've received unexpected invoices or correspondence that you have no idea how to handle, we provide free guidance and support to our Medigap and Medicare Advantage policyholders. Learn more about what we offer at no cost to you:

https://boomerbenefits.com/faq/why-do-i-need-an-agent/
https://boomerbenefits.com/client-service-team/

It's Not too Late

What can you do if you signed up for Medicare before you read this book and didn't have the benefit of knowing the answers to so many questions? Is it too late to work with an independent agency like Boomer Benefits that provides the kind of back-end support that you may now realize you need?

Perhaps not, so please reach out. Remember, it costs nothing to get help from an independent agent or broker. If you can pass underwriting, we can help you find a smart move that benefits you and also allows us to represent you. Likewise, if you chose a Medicare Advantage plan and wish that you had chosen a Medigap plan instead, or vice versa, we may be able to find a valid election period that can help you with going the other route. However, if we find that you are already enrolled in the right plan for you, we'll tell you that, too, and advise you to sit tight.

Federal Government Resources

You may have questions about your own benefits that only Medicare or Social Security can answer. Here is how you can reach them:

The Centers for Medicare and Medicaid Services
1-800-MEDICARE
TTY 1-877-486-2048
www.medicare.gov

Contact Medicare for questions regarding your coverage and claims. Medicare tracks your enrollment into both Medicare Advantage and Part D plans and can help you with details about what you are currently enrolled in.

Social Security Administration
1-800-772-1213
TTY 1-800-325-0778
www.ssa.gov

Contact Social Security for questions regarding enrollment into Medicare and your premiums for Medicare. Social Security is also where you can apply for the Extra Help for Part D program (low-income subsidy).

Glossary

Annual Election Period

The period that runs from October 15 – December 7 each year during which Medicare beneficiaries can enroll in, change, or disenroll from a Medicare Advantage plan or Part D drug plan.

Annual Notice of Change (ANOC)

The ANOC letter is a notice that Medicare Advantage and Part D plans must send their members each September that outlines the changes to their plan for the coming year. It may include increases or decreases to benefits, premiums, copays, and insurance. It may also include additions or deletions from the plan's drug formulary for the following year.

Assignment

When a provider accepts "Medicare assignment" or "Medicare's assigned rates," it means he or she has agreed to accept Medicare's payment for your health-care service as payment in full. No balance billing is allowed.

Attained-Age Rating

Some Medigap insurance companies price their plans based

on the age at which you applied for the policy. This is called the *Attained-Age Rating* method.

Beneficiary

A person who receives his or her health-care coverage through Medicare.

Benefit Period

Under Medicare Part A, a *Benefit Period* begins with the day you are admitted into the hospital and lasts until 60 days after you have been discharged from the hospital or a skilled-nursing facility.

Catastrophic Coverage Limit

Under Medicare Part D, the *Catastrophic Coverage Limit* kicks in after a Medicare beneficiary has spent a certain number of dollars each year. Once you have reached the catastrophic coverage level of your Part D drug plan, the plan must pay 95% of the cost of your covered medications for the remainder of the year.

Claim

A request for direct payment or reimbursement from Medicare or another health insurance provider for covered medical services.

Consolidated Omnibus Budget Reconciliation Act (COBRA)

COBRA insurance offers retirees an opportunity to extend

their former employer health coverage for a number of months after they have retired, at their own expense.

Coinsurance

The percentage that you must pay toward your own covered health-care services.

Community Rating

A rating class used by Medigap companies in which age is not a factor in determining your monthly premiums. Within the community, beneficiaries pay the same monthly rate regardless of their age.

Copay

A *copay* is a set dollar amount that you must pay toward the cost of your covered health-care services. For example, it's common for insurance companies to require a copay when you visit the doctor or fill a prescription.

Cost-Sharing

The amount of money that you are required to pay as your share of the cost of a medical service. Deductibles, copays, and coinsurance are all examples of *cost-sharing*.

Coverage Gap

Sometimes called the "Donut Hole," the *Coverage Gap* occurs when your total cost of prescription medications reaches a certain dollar limit that is set each year by Medicare. During the gap, the cost that you pay toward your medications may change. You continue paying the new cost until your total out-of-pocket drug spending reaches the Part D catastrophic coverage limit.

Creditable Coverage

Insurance coverage that is equal to or better than your coverage from another source. For example, employer coverage from a large employer with 20 or more employees is considered *creditable coverage* that allows you to delay enrollment into Parts B and D without penalty.

Custodial Care

Nonskilled medical care designed to help a person with daily living activities like eating, dressing, bathing, transferring, and toileting.

Deductible

The amount of money that you must spend out-of-pocket toward your covered medical expenses before the insurance plan begins to pay benefits.

Drug Tier

Medications on a Part D drug formulary are grouped into tiers that determine your portion of the drug cost. For example, Tier 1 usually includes preferred generic medications.

Dual Eligible

When a Medicare beneficiary qualifies for both Medicare and Medicaid, he or she is considered "dual eligible."

Durable Medical Equipment

Medical equipment that is ordered or prescribed by a doctor or other Medicare provider for your use. Examples are crutches, hospital beds, oxygen equipment, canes, walkers, and wheelchairs.

End-Stage Renal Disease (ESRD)

A chronic kidney disease in which the kidneys fail to filter waste and excess fluid from the blood. People with ESRD usually require dialysis or may need a kidney transplant.

Evidence of Coverage (EOC)

A list of costs and covered services under your Medicare Advantage or Part D drug plan. Your insurance company must send you the EOC whenever you enroll in or renew your coverage.

Excess Charge

Under Part B, nonparticipating Medicare providers can charge up to 15% more than what Medicare will pay for a covered service. This is called a *Part B Excess Charge*.

Extra Help for Part D Program

Also called the *Low-Income Subsidy*, this is a federal program to help reduce the costs of medications under Part D for certain low-income Medicare beneficiaries.

Formulary

A list of medications that are covered under a Part D plan.

Formulary Exception

A request whereby a Medicare plan member (and his or her doctor) asks the plan to cover a drug that is not on the formulary or to cover the drug without certain restrictions.

General Enrollment Period (GEP)

The GEP runs from January 1 to March 31 each year. It is a time when you can sign up for Medicare Parts A and/or B if you missed your Initial Enrollment Period. Your coverage will begin the following July 1.

Guaranteed-Issue (GI)

Rights that you have in certain situations to enroll in Medigap coverage without underwriting. The insurance company must sell you the policy and cover any preexisting conditions when you enroll during a valid GI window.

Guaranteed Renewable

Insurance coverage that cannot be terminated or rated-up by the insurance company due to any new health conditions that you may experience. For example, a Medigap plan is *guaranteed renewable.* The carrier can only cancel your policy if you fail to pay your premiums beyond the grace period.

Health Maintenance Organization (HMO)

A type of managed care network that is commonly found in Medicare Advantage plans. Most HMO plans will require you to designate a primary care physician and you may need referrals to see a specialist.

Home Health Care

Health-care services covered by Medicare that are delivered to you in your own home. This may include skilled-nursing care, physical therapy, speech therapy, and home health aide services, among other things. Certain conditions must be met to qualify for most home health care.

Hospice Care

End-of-life care that focuses on quality of life and pain management of symptoms. Medicare covers hospice care under Part A when a doctor certifies that you are terminally ill with a life expectancy of no more than 6 months.

Household Discount

A discount on your monthly insurance premiums for meeting certain requirements, such as being married to someone who also has insurance with the same insurance company.

Individual Health Insurance Plan

Health insurance coverage that an individual under age 65 can purchase for him- or herself or his or her family through the ACA Marketplace or health-care exchange.

Initial Coverage Phase

Under Part D, the *Initial Coverage Phase* is the coverage phase that follows the annual deductible. During initial coverage, you will pay copays or coinsurance for your medications as set by the insurance company providing the drug coverage.

Initial Enrollment Period

A seven-month window during which individuals newly eligible for Medicare can sign up for Medicare Parts A, B, C, or D. You become eligible for Medicare at 65, though some people qualify early due to disability.

Inpatient Care

Medical care that you receive after being admitted to a hospital or skilled-nursing facility.

IRMAA

The Income Related Monthly Adjustment Amount is an additional monthly premium that people with certain high-income levels must pay for Medicare Parts B and D.

Issue-Age Rating

A rating class in which a Medigap insurance company

determines the rate based on the age at which you purchase your policy.

Late-Enrollment Penalty

A fee that is added to your monthly Medicare premium for failing to enroll in Medicare when you were first eligible. Once incurred, the fee lasts as long as you are enrolled in Medicare, which is usually the rest of your life.

Lifetime Reserve Days

A bank of 60 inpatient hospital days that you can use only once per lifetime. Under Medicare Part A, you would use your lifetime reserve days for any hospital coverage beyond the first 90 days in a given benefit period.

Long-Term Care

Non-medical services provided to someone who is unable to manage his or her own basic activities of daily living such as eating, dressing, bathing, and toileting. This care can be provided in your own home or at a long-term-care facility such as an assisted-living home or nursing home. Medicare does not cover long-term-care expenses.

Maximum Out-of-Pocket Limit (MOOP)

The MOOP is the most that you will need to pay toward covered Part A and B services in any one calendar year while enrolled in a Medicare Advantage plan. It includes any deductible spending, copays, and coinsurance that you spend. It does not include monthly premiums.

Medicaid

A joint state and federal program to provide health care for low-income individuals. People who qualify for Medicaid may get assistance with paying their Parts B and D premiums, deductibles, copays, and coinsurance.

Medicare Advantage

Also known as *Part C*, the *Medicare Advantage* program is a form of managed care that allows Medicare beneficiaries to get their Parts A and B benefits through a private insurance plan and its network or providers. Many Medicare Advantage plans offer a built-in Part D drug plan.

Medicare Cost Plan

A type of Medicare health plan that offers its members both a network of doctors and hospitals as well as the ability to seek treatment with non-network providers under Original Medicare.

Medicare Medical Savings Plan (MSA)

A type of Medicare Advantage plan that combines a high-deductible health plan with a medical savings account. These plans have networks of providers but do not include Part D drug coverage.

Medicare Savings Programs

State programs that use Medicaid funds to help eligible low-income individuals pay for some or all of their out-of-pocket expenses under Medicare.

Medicare SELECT Plan

A type of Medigap plan that operates a network of hospitals. Policyholders must seek treatment at these hospitals for their care to be covered.

Medicare Summary Notice (MSN)

The quarterly explanation of benefits statement that Medicare provides to show you the health-care services received and what Medicare paid toward them. You should review your MSN to determine if you owe any balances that are due.

Medically Necessary

Health-care services are medically necessary when needed to diagnose or treat an injury, illness, or disease under Medicare's guidelines.

Medigap Open Enrollment Period (Medigap OEP)

A period during which you can purchase any Medigap plan without medical underwriting. It begins with your Part B effective date and lasts for six months.

Medigap Plan

Also called a *Medicare Supplement*, a *Medigap plan* is a private insurance policy that you can purchase to help you pay for the deductibles, copays, and coinsurance not covered by Medicare.

Open Enrollment Period

Another term for the Annual Election Period that runs from October 15 – December 7.

Original Medicare

A term that refers to Medicare Parts A and B together as they were designed when created in 1965. Beneficiaries with Original Medicare get their coverage from the federal government as opposed to a Medicare Advantage plan. Also referred to as *Traditional Medicare.*

Part A

Medicare *Part A* covers inpatient hospital stays, blood transfusions, skilled nursing, home-health services, and hospice care.

Part B

Medicare *Part B* covers outpatient medical services, including preventive care, visits to your doctors, lab testing, and more.

Part C

The Medicare Advantage program is also referred to as *Part C* of Medicare.

Part D

Voluntary prescription drug coverage that is available either through a Medicare Advantage plan or through a standalone *Part D* plan.

Preferred Provider Organization (PPO)

Another type of managed care network that is commonly operated by Medicare Advantage plans. PPO plans have flexible networks, meaning that you can see out-of-network providers at an additional cost to you.

Private Fee for Service (PFFS)

A Medicare *Private Fee for Service Plan* is a type of Medicare Advantage plan that allows you to be treated by any doctor who is willing to accept the plan's terms and bill the plan for your treatment. PFFS plans are not typically found in areas where two or more network Medicare Advantage plans operate, so they can be hard to find.

Premium

A monthly expense that you pay to an insurance carrier in exchange for coverage of your health risk.

Prescription Drug

A medicine that is prescribed by a doctor and is generally not available over the counter.

Preventive Care

Screening tests and other care that is provided to prevent

illness or disease. Many of Medicare's preventive care services are covered 100%.

Primary Care Physician (PCP)

A family care doctor or internist that you select to be your primary physician when you enroll in certain Medicare Advantage plans. Under a Medicare HMO plan, this doctor must write a referral for you to see a specialist.

Primary Coverage

The health insurance coverage that pays first when you have more than one type of medical coverage.

Prior Authorization

An approval that you must get from your Part D insurance company before it will cover a medication. This usually involves additional paperwork that the insurance company will ask of your doctor as to why you need this medication.

Quantity Limit

A limit to the dosage or quantity that an insurance company will cover for certain medications.

Secondary Coverage

The health insurance coverage that pays after the primary coverage first pays when you have more than one type of coverage.

Service Area

The area in which a Medicare Advantage plan offers its network coverage. You must live in a Medicare Advantage's plan service area to be eligible to enroll.

Skilled-Nursing Facility

An inpatient rehabilitation center where Medicare beneficiaries can go for continuing health care, usually after a hospital stay. An SNF is staffed with a variety of medical professionals to aid in the recovery of its patients.

Special Election Periods

Certain times when a Medicare beneficiary is allowed an exception to enroll or disenroll in a Medicare Advantage or Prescription Drug plan outside of the Initial Enrollment Period or Annual Election Period.

Special Enrollment Period

Certain times when a Medicare beneficiary is allowed an exception to enroll in Medicare outside of the normal Initial Enrollment Period.

Special Needs Plans

A type of Medicare Advantage plan that is designed to assist beneficiaries who have a specific qualifying chronic illness or who have both Medicare and Medicaid. *Special Needs Plans* also exist for people who live in institutions.

Standalone Part D Plan

Drug coverage that you can purchase to go alongside your Original Medicare and Medicare Supplement benefits.

Step Therapy

A restriction that an insurance company places on a medication that requires the patient to first try an alternative and less expensive medication before the plan will cover the more expensive medication.

Trial Right SEP

Under a Medicare Advantage plan, you have a one-time *Trial Right* to leave your coverage during the first 12 months and return to Medicare and/or your prior Medigap company. Your Trial Right allows you to enroll or reenroll in a Medigap plan without medical underwriting.

TRICARE for Life (TFL)

Health Insurance coverage that pays secondary to Medicare for eligible retired service members and their family members. TFL functions as a wraparound or supplemental coverage to Medicare.

True Out-of-Pocket (TrOOP)

Your *TrOOP* is the total out-of-pocket costs that you spend during a calendar year on covered medications that are listed in your Part D plan's formulary. Once you reach your

TrOOP, you will move into the catastrophic coverage phase of your plan.

Underwriting

A process used by insurance companies to assess the financial risk of taking you on as an insured member. Underwriters will review your answers to medical questions as well as your medical records to determine whether the company will offer you coverage.

Acknowledgments

Dear Reader,

I've done my very best to provide accurate information and eliminate such annoying and pesky things as typos in this book. However, if you find a mistake or error, I welcome you to reach out to me at the book's website: https://tenmedicaremistakes. com. We will update the book annually with all the latest Medicare numbers, so your constructive feedback is most welcome. It will help us improve future versions of the book.

Over the last 15 years educating people about Medicare, I've had many people suggest that I write a book. While many people watch our YouTube videos or sign up for our online email courses, there's just something about having a book in your hands – something you can highlight and make notes in – that appeals to many people. I'm a voracious reader myself, so I know this well.

However, there are already several books about Medicare basics available. I wasn't convinced that the market really needed another Medicare 101 book.

Then one day a member of our team said something which sparked an idea. She pointed out that Medicare beneficiaries across America all tend to make the *same enrollment mistakes*. She wished there were a better way to warn them all about the most common missteps before they turn 65.

From a business perspective, common Medicare mistakes are

not a bad thing because it makes us valuable to our policyholders. We know and recognize these pitfalls and we can use that knowledge to help our own clients avoid the dangers.

However, with more than 10,000 baby boomers aging into Medicare every day, millions of beneficiaries out there are not our clients and, therefore, will never benefit from that information.

With that in mind, I set to work on a book for the general public that identifies and describes the usual Medicare mistakes that we see beneficiaries make time and again. While it has been a monumental effort, writing this book for you has also been most rewarding, knowing that it can make your entry into Medicare easier.

Along the way, I had quite a bit of help. Many thanks to Valaree Gray, Crystal Millican, Kelsey Mundfrom, Bailey Sigmon, and Corey Hammonds for reading the early drafts of the book and helping me to expand and improve it. Thanks also to our amazing web developer, Brian Patman, for designing the book's website.

I must also thank our very dedicated group of beta readers who came up with so many great suggestions, stories, and examples that have helped me to make the book a more relevant reading experience. I'm indebted to each of you who stayed with me through each chapter release to help me write a better book: Becky Coleman, Julia Cohen Sandler, Mary Berger, Tom Serface Louise Reed, Rebecca Sue, Deborah Campbell, Terrie Watson, Simon Lia, Russ Harrison, Diana Feil, Nancy Kaine, Loretta Ann, Djean Overbey. Beverly Beckon, Maryanne Sheehan Kelleher, Robert Nasso, Barbalee Blair, Nancy Pendleton, Terry Crabtree, Tim Irby, and Vickie Sanford.

To the many people at the Centers for Medicare and Medicaid Services (CMS) who every day help Medicare beneficiaries interpret and apply all of Medicare's rules and regulations, I must say that we have come across so many of you who truly care about our nation's beneficiaries and are dedicated to helping them understand their coverage. We owe you a debt of thanks for doing the job that you do.

I'd like to thank the extraordinary people at the Kaiser Family Foundation, whose website I have consulted hundreds of times for facts, analysis, statistics, and wisdom about Medicare over the last decade. The amount of time and effort you put into providing accurate information for the public is astonishing and so appreciated.

Another great resource who continually keeps agents like me in "the know" about Medicare is Ron Iverson of the National Association of Medicare Supplement and Medicare Advantage Producers, Inc. (NAMSMAP). Ron produces a truly phenomenal newsletter for Medicare insurance agents that I have come to depend on.

It goes without saying that any good book must have a good editor and a good designer, so many thanks to Madalyn Stone and Jerry Dorris for your expert work.

To the thousands of policyholders who have trusted me or someone on my team to guide you in your Medicare decisions, there are no words to express how often you inspire me and make me grateful to work with people like you.

To my husband, Greg Roberts, thanks for sticking by me through the long hours that I have put into my business and into this book. I know that Medicare is not a very exciting subject for a Canadian citizen who only recently became a resident of the United States, but I appreciate how you are always willing to be my sounding board.

Lastly, I'd to thank my mother, Sharon, for believing in my writing ability since my first published article in the 2nd grade, and my brother, David, who has worked together with me for fifteen years to build an agency that we can be proud of.

About the Author

Danielle Kunkle Roberts is the co-founder of Boomer Benefits, a health insurance agency that helps baby boomers and seniors navigate Medicare and select suitable supplemental coverage in 49 states. She and her team have helped more than 50,000 beneficiaries with their decisions about Medicare since 2005. You can read more than 5,000 five-star reviews about her agency online. Danielle has appeared on over 100 podcasts, radio shows, and television news segments to offer enrollment advice and education on Medicare.

She is a member of the Forbes Finance Council and past president of the Fort Worth chapter of the National Association of Health Underwriters (NAHU), where she also served two years on the Texas Association of Health Underwriters (TAHU) state board as their magazine editor. She currently serves as the TAHU Medicare chairperson. She lives in Fort Worth, Texas with her husband and two adorable and scruffy fur-kids.

Notes

Chapter 1

1. Juliette Cubanksi, Anthony Damico, and Tricia Neuman, "10 Things to Know About Medicare Part D Coverage and Costs in 2019," Kaiser Family Foundation, June 4, 2019, https://www.kff.org/medicare/issue-brief/10-things-to-know-about-medicare-part-d-coverage-and-costs-in-2019/

2. Juliette Cubanski, Tricia Neuman, Anthony Damico, and Karen Smith. "Medicare Beneficiaries' Out-of-Pocket Health Care Spending as a Share of Income Now and Projections for the Future," Kaiser Family Foundation, January 26, 2018, https://www.kff.org/medicare/report/medicare-beneficiaries-out-of-pocket-health-care-spending-as-a-share-of-income-now-and-projections-for-the-future/

3. 2020 "Social Security Fact Sheet," https://www.ssa.gov/news/press/factsheets/basicfact-alt.pdf

4. Juliette Cubanski and Tricia Neuman, Kaiser Family Foundation, "Medicare's Income-Related Premiums Under Current Law and Changes for 2019," Kaiser Family Foundation, October 31, 2018, https://www.kff.org/medicare/issue-brief/medicares-income-related-premiums-under-current-law-and-changes-for-2019/

5. Juliette Cubanski and Anthony Damico, "Medicare Part D: A First Look at Medicare Prescription Drug Plans in 2021,"

6. Kaiser Family Foundation, October 29, 2020, https://www.kff.org/medicare/issue-brief/medicare-part-d-a-first-look-at-medicare-prescription-drug-plans-in-2021/

Chapter 2

1. Kevin J. Contrera, Margaret I. Wallhagen, Sara K. Mamo, Esther S. Oh, and Frank R. Lin, "Hearing Loss Health Care for Older Adults," *Journal of the American Board of Family Medicine, Vol. 29 No.3*, May-June 2016, https://www.jabfm.org/content/jabfp/29/3/394.full.pdf

2. "Most Medicare Beneficiaries Lack Dental Coverage, and Many Go Without Needed Care," Kaiser Family Foundation, March 13, 2019, https://www.kff.org/medicare/press-release/most-medicare-beneficiaries-lack-dental-coverage-and-many-go-without-needed-care

3. Costs of Care, LongTermCare.gov, U.S. Department of Health and Human Services, 2016, https://longtermcare.acl.gov/costs-how-to-pay/costs-of-care.html

4. Selena Maranjian, "5 Long-Term Care Stats That Will Blow You Away," The Motley Fool, September 2, 2018, https://www.fool.com/retirement/2018/09/02/5-long-term-care-stats-that-will-blow-you-away.aspx

Chapter 4

1. Juliette Cubanksi, Anthony Damico, and Tricia Neuman, "10 Things to Know About Medicare Part D Coverage and Costs in 2019," Kaiser Family Foundation, June 4, 2019, https://www.kff.org/medicare/issue-brief/10-things-to-know-about-medicare-part-d-coverage-and-costs-in-2019/

2. Juliette Cubanski, Wyatt Koma, and Tricia Neuman, "The Out of Pocket Cost Burden for Specialty Drugs in Medicare Part D in 2019," Kaiser Family Foundation, Feb 1, 2019, https://www.kff.org/report-section/the-out-of-pocket-cost-burden-for-specialty-drugs-in-medicare-part-d-in-2019-findings/

Chapter 6

1. Juliette Cubanski, Tricia Neuman, Gretchen Jacobson, Cristina Boccuti, "What Are the Implications of Repealing the Affordable Care Act for Medicare Spending and Beneficiaries?" Kaiser Family Foundation, December 13, 2016, https://www.kff.org/health-reform/issue-brief/what-are-the-implications-of-repealing-the-affordable-care-act-for-medicare-spending-and-beneficiaries/

2. Juliette Cubanksi, Tricia, Neuman, Meredith Freed, "The Facts on Medicare Spending and Financing, Kaiser Family Foundation, August 20, 2019, https://www.kff.org/medicare/issue-brief/the-facts-on-medicare-spending-and-financing/

3. Virgil Dickson, Modern Healthcare, "Fewer doctors are opting out of Medicare," January 30, 2018, https://www.modernhealthcare.com/article/20180130/NEWS/180139995/fewer-doctors-are-opting-out-of-medicare

4. Cristina Boccuti, Christa Fields, GiselleCasillas, Liz Hamel, "Primary Care Physicians Accepting Medicare: A Snapshot," Kaiser Family Foundation, October 30, 2015, https://www.kff.org/medicare/issue-brief/primary-care-physicians-accepting-medicare-a-snapshot/

5. State of Medigap 2019: Trends in Enrollment and Demographics, AHIP, May 2019, https://www.ahip.org/wp-content/uploads/IB_StateofMedigap2019.pdf

Chapter 7

1. Christie Teigland, Zulkarnain Pulungan, Tanya Shah, Eric C. Schneider, and Shawn Bishop, "As It Grows, Medicare Advantage is Enrolling More Low-Income and Medically Complex Beneficiaries: Recent Trends in Beneficiary Clinical Characteristics, Health Care Utilization, and Spending, The Commonwealth Fund, May 2020, https://www.commonwealthfund.org/sites/default/files/2020-05/Teigland_Medicare_Advantage_beneficiary_trends_ib.pdf

2. Meredith Free, Anthony Damico, and Tricia Neuman, " A Dozen Facts About Medicare Advantage in 2020," Kaiser Family Foundation, April 22, 2020, https://www.kff.org/medicare/issue-brief/a-dozen-facts-about-medicare-advantage-in-2020/

3. Jeanne Fuglesten Biniek, Meredith Freed, Anthony Damico, Tricia Neuman, "Medicare Advantage 2021 Spotlight: First Look," Kaiser Family Foundation, October 29, 2020, https://www.kff.org/medicare/issue-brief/medicare-advantage-2021-spotlight-first-look/

4. Meredith Free, Anthony Damico, and Tricia Neuman, " A Dozen Facts About Medicare Advantage in 2020," Kaiser Family Foundation, April 22, 2020, https://www.kff.org/medicare/issue-brief/a-dozen-facts-about-medicare-advantage-in-2020/

5. Gretchen Jacobson, Meredith Free, Antony Damico, Tricia Newman, "A Dozen Facts About Medicare Advantage in 2019," Kaiser Family Foundation, June 6, 2019, https://www.kff.org/medicare/issue-brief/a-dozen-facts-about-medicare-advantage-in-2019/

6. Meredith Free, Anthony Damico, and Tricia Neuman, " A Dozen Facts About Medicare Advantage in 2020," Kaiser Family Foundation, April 22, 2020, https://www.kff.org/medicare/issue-brief/a-dozen-facts-about-medicare-advantage-in-2020/

Chapter 10

1. Tara Bishop, Matthew J. Press, Salomeh Keyhani, "Acceptance of Insurance by Psychiatrists and the Implications for Access to Mental Health Care," JAMA Psychiatry, February 2014
2. https://jamanetwork.com/journals/jamapsychiatry/fullarticle/1785174
3. National Association of Insurance Commissioners, "NAIC Medicare Supplement Insurance Model Regulation Compliance Manual," January 2019, https://www.naic.org/documents/prod_serv_supplementary_med_lm.pdf
4. Wyatt Koma, Juliette Cubanski, Gretchen Jacobson, Anthony Damico, Tricia Neuman, "No Itch to Switch: Few Medicare Beneficiaries Switch Plans During the Open Enrollment Period," Kaiser Family Foundation, December 2, 2019, https://www.kff.org/medicare/issue-brief/no-itch-to-switch-few-medicare-beneficiaries-switch-plans-during-the-open-enrollment-period/